PASSWORDS

to English 3

Michaela Blackledge
Joanna Crewe
Jane Flintoft
Julia Waines

OXFORD
UNIVERSITY PRESS

OXFORD
UNIVERSITY PRESS

Great Clarendon Street, Oxford OX2 6DP

Oxford University Press is a department of the University of Oxford.
It furthers the University's objective of excellence in research,
scholarship, and education by publishing worldwide in

Oxford New York

Auckland Bangkok Buenos Aires Cape Town Chennai
Dar es Salaam Delhi Hong Kong Istanbul Karachi Kolkata
Kuala Lumpur Madrid Melbourne Mexico City Mumbai
Nairobi São Paulo Shanghai Taipei Tokyo Toronto

Oxford is a registered trade mark of Oxford University Press
in the UK and in certain other countries

British Library Cataloguing in Publication Data

Data available

ISBN 0 19 832090 6

10 9 8 7 6 5 4 3 2 1

Printed in Italy by Rotolito Lombarda.

Acknowledgements
We are grateful for permission to reproduce the following copyright
material:

John Agard: 'Half-Caste' from *Get Back Pimple* (Viking, 1996), reprinted
by permission of the author c/o Caroline Sheldon Literary Agency.
Simon Armitage: 'I am very bothered when I think' from *Book of Matches*
(1993), reprinted by permission of the publishers, Faber & Faber Ltd.
Christina Dodwell: extract from 'The Sepik and the Waghi', copyright ©
Christine Dodwell 1984, first published in *River Journeys* introduced by
Roger Laughton (BBC Books, 1984), reprinted by permission of the author.
Roland Fiddy: cartoon from *The Victim's Guide to the Dentist* (Exley, 1993),
copyright © Roland Fiddy 1993, reprinted by permission of Exley
Publications Ltd.
Christine Green: extract from *Get Fit for Summer* (Parragon, 2000),
reprinted by permission of the publishers.
Alvin Hall: extract from *Money for Life - Everyone's Guide to Financial
Freedom* (2000), reprinted by permission of the publishers, Hodder &
Stoughton Ltd.
Pete McCarthy: extract from *McCarthy's Bar: a journey of discovery in
Ireland* (2000), reprinted by permission of the publishers, Hodder &
Stoughton Ltd.
R K Narayan: 'The Watchman' from *Under the Banyan Tree and Other
Stories* (Heinemann, 1985), reprinted by permission of The Random House
Group Ltd.
Jamie Oliver: extract from *The Return of the Naked Chef* (Michael Joseph,
2000), copyright © Jamie Oliver 2000, reprinted by permission of Penguin
Books Ltd.
J R R Tolkien: opening of *Lord of the Rings: The Fellowship of the Ring*
(HarperCollins, 1991), copyright © George Allen & Unwin 1954, reprinted
by permission of HarperCollins Publishers Ltd.

John Wiseman: extract from *SAS Survival Handbook* (Collins Harvill,
1986) copyright © John Wiseman 1986, reprinted by permission of
HarperCollins Publishers Ltd.

and also to the following for their permission to use copyright material

The Guardian Media Group for review of J R R Tolkien: *Lord of the
Rings: The Fellowship of the Ring*, used on cover of HarperCollins edition.
Oxford University Press for extracts from *MacBeth* edited by Roma Gill
(Oxford School Shakespeare, 2001).
Seven Seas Ltd for product information from www.multibionta.co.uk
World Wide Fund for Nature (WWF) for article from
www.worldwildlife.org

We regret we have been unable to trace and contact all copyright holders
of material included before publication. If notified the publisher
undertakes to rectify any errors or omissions at the earliest opportunity.

The Publisher would like to thank the following for permission to
reproduce photographs:

Alamy Images: p 78; Donald Cooper/Photostage: pp 43, 44 (bottom);
Corbis/Bettmann: pp 42, 62; Corbis/Wolfgang Kaehler: p 108; Corbis/Amos
Nachoum: p 101; Corbis/Reflections Photolibrary/Jennie Woodcock: p 88;
Corbis/Reuters: p 61; Corbis/Reuters/Mike Finn-Kelcy: p 72; Corbis/Royalty
Free: pp 32, 85; Hemera Photo Objects: pp 35, 44 (top); Heritage Image
Partnership: p 86; Ingram Publishing: pp 75, 109; Movie Store: pp 15, 23;
Oxford University Press: p 119; Photodisc: pp 19, 97; Rex Features: pp 40,
117; Stockbyte: pp 74, 104; Mahesh Venkitachalam: pp 6, 8.
Logos: British Airways, Domino Pizzas; Penguin Books, The Post Office;
Shell.

Cover photo: Hemera

Artwork is by John Adams, Kathy Baxendale; Ruth Galloway, Bill
Greenhead, Sarah Horne, Peter Melnycuk, Richard Morris, Matthew
Robson and Mark Nesbitt/Luke Warm.

Icons by Tim Kahane

Contents

Introduction

Welcome to *Passwords to English*!

Passwords can open up exciting new places. This book will take you into the world of English. You will read about a society controlled by Big Brother, a potion that turns a doctor into a murderous beast, shark attacks, a power-hungry wife persuading her husband to kill the king, and get to write about the things that interest *you*!

Look for these symbols to help you:

 This means there's a text for you to read.

 This means there's a starter activity to do.

Password	Audience	
	The **audience** is the people who read the text.	

Key things you need to know and understand are explained.

 This section helps you to remember what you have learnt.

 This means it is your turn to think about your own text.

 This means to start writing!

→ Remember!

Persuasive texts may use:
► repetition
► exaggeration
► rhetorical questions
► imperatives.

Use the Remember panels to remind yourself of the main points in each unit. At the back of the book is a quiz that you can use with a partner!

There's lots to do in this book, as well as lots to read, talk and write about. So turn the pages and enjoy it!

Michaela Blackledge
Joanna Crewe
Jane Flintoft
Julia Waines

Narratives: time and place

In this unit you will:

➤ explore writing from different cultures, traditions and times
➤ investigate the way ideas, values and emotions can be presented
➤ look at words and their meanings
➤ identify some themes.

Get started

It is important to look for layers of meaning in a narrative. Think about the fable of the wolf in sheep's clothing: a wolf puts on a sheepskin and approaches some sheep. A lamb falls for the disguise and follows the wolf, which then gobbles him up. This story is not just about a wolf dressing up. It is about how what you see is not always what you get.

With a partner, make a list of stories that have layers of meaning. (Hint: think about other fables, religious stories, etc.)

'The Watchman'

This short story is called 'The Watchman' and belongs to a collection called 'Under the Banyan Tree'. The author, R.K. Narayan, is a well-known storyteller in his country – India. He sets his stories in a fictional Indian town called Malgudi.

In 'The Watchman', the main character – a watchman – meets a young girl who is unhappy with her life. They talk, but the watchman cannot really understand why the girl is sad. After this meeting, the watchman often thinks about the girl, until one day – years later – he sees her again.

There was still a faint splash of red on the western horizon. The watchman stood on the tank bund and took a final survey. All the people who had come for evening walks had returned to their homes. Not a soul anywhere – except that obstinate angler, at the northern end, who sat with his feet in water, sadly gazing on his rod. It was no use bothering about him: he would sit there till midnight, hoping for a catch.

The Taluk office gong struck nine. The watchman was satisfied that no trespassing cattle had sneaked in through the wire fencing. As he turned to go, he saw, about a hundred yards away, a shadowy figure moving down the narrow stone steps that led to the water's edge. He thought for a second that it might be a ghost. He dismissed the idea, and went up to investigate. If it was anyone come to bathe at this hour ... From the top step he observed that it was a woman's form. She stooped over the last step and placed something on it – possibly a letter. She then stepped into knee-deep water, and stood there, her hands pressed together in prayer. Unmistakeable signs – always to be followed by the police and gruesome details, bringing the very worst possible reputation to a tank.

He shouted, 'Come out, there, come out of it.' The form looked up from the water. 'Don't stand there and gaze. You'll catch a cold, come up whoever you are ...' He raced down the steps and picked up the letter. He hurriedly lit his lamp, and turned its wick till it burnt brightly, and held it up, murmuring: 'I don't like this. Why is everyone coming to the same tank? If you want to be dead, throw yourself under an engine,' he said.

The light fell on the other's face. It was a young girl's, wet with tears. He felt a sudden pity. He said, 'Sit down, sit down and rest ... no, no ... go up two more steps and sit down. Don't sit so near the water ...' She obeyed. He sat down on the last step between her and the water, placed the lantern on the step, took out a piece of tobacco, and put it in his mouth. She buried her face in her hands, and began to sob. He felt troubled and asked: 'Why don't you rise and go home, lady?'

She spluttered through her sob: 'I have no home in this world!'

'Don't tell me! Surely, you didn't grow up without a home all these years!' said the watchman.

'I lost my mother when I was five years old –' she said.

'I thought so ...' replied the watchman, and added, 'and your father married again and you grew up under the care of your stepmother?'

'Yes, yes, how do you know?' she asked.

'I am sixty-five years old,' he said and asked, 'Did your stepmother trouble you?'

'No, there you are wrong,' the girl said. 'She is very kind to me. She has been looking after me ever since my father died a few years ago. She has just a little money on hand left by my father, and she spends it on us.'

The watchman looked at the stars, sighed for the dinner that he was missing. 'It's very late, madam, go home.'

'I tell you I've no home–' she retorted angrily.

'Your stepmother's house is all right from what you say. She is good to you.'

'But why should I be a burden to her? Who am I?'

'You are her husband's daughter,' the watchman said, and added, 'That is enough claim.'

'No, no. I won't live on anybody's charity.'

'Then you will have to wait till they find you a husband–'

She glared at him in the dark. 'That's what I do not want to do. I want to study and become a doctor and earn my livelihood. I don't want to marry. I often catch my mother talking far into the night with her eldest son, worrying about my future, about my marriage. I know they cannot afford to keep me in college very long now; it costs about twenty rupees a month.'

'Twenty rupees!' the watchman exclaimed. It was his month's salary. 'How can anybody spend so much for books!'

'Till today,' she said, 'I was hoping that I would get a scholarship. That would have saved me. But this evening they announced; others have got it, not I. My name is not there –' and she broke down again. The watchman looked at her in surprise. He comprehended very little of all this situation. She added: 'And when they come to know of this, they will try to arrange my marriage. Someone is coming to have a look at me tomorrow.'

'Marry him and may God bless you with ten children.'

'No, no,' she cried hysterically. 'I don't want to marry. I want to study.'

The silent night was stabbed by her sobbing and some night bird rustled the water, and wavelets beat upon the shore. Seeing her suffer, he found his own sorrows in life came to his mind; how in those far-off times, in his little village home an epidemic of cholera laid out his father and mother and brothers on the same day, and he was the sole survivor; how he was turned out of his ancestral home through the trickery of his father's kinsmen, and he wandered as an orphan, suffering indescribable hunger and privation.

'Everyone has his own miseries,' he said. 'If people tried to kill themselves for each one of them, I don't know how often they would have to drown.' He remembered further incidents and his voice shook with sorrow. 'You are young and you don't know what sorrow is ...' He remained silent and a sob broke out of him as he said: 'I prayed to all the gods in the world for a son. My wife bore me eight children. Only one daughter lives now, and none of the others saw the eleventh year...' The girl looked at him in bewilderment.

The Taluk office gong struck again. 'It is late, you had better get up and go home,' he said.

She replied: 'I have no home.'

He felt irritated. 'You are making too much of nothing. You should not be obstinate –'

'You don't know my trouble,' she said.

He picked up his lantern and staff and got up. He put her letter down where he found it.

'If you are going to be so obstinate, I'll leave you alone. No one can blame me.' He paused for a moment, looked at her, and went up the steps; not a word passed between them again.

The moment he came back to duty next morning, he hurried down the stone steps. The letter lay where he had dropped it the previous night. He picked it up and gazed on it, helplessly, wishing that it could tell him about the fate of the girl after he had left her. He tore it up and flung it on the water. As he watched the bits float off on ripples, he blamed himself for leaving her and going away on the previous night. 'I am responsible for at least one suicide in this tank,' he often remarked to himself. He could never look at the blue expanse of water again with an easy mind. Even many months later he could not be certain that the remains of a body would not come up all of a sudden. 'Who knows, it sometimes happens that the body gets stuck deep down,' he reflected.

Years later, one evening as he stood on the bund and took a final survey before going home, he saw a car draw up on the road below. A man, a woman, and three children emerged from the car and climbed the bund. When they approached, the watchman felt a start at his heart; the figure and the face of the woman seemed familiar to him. Though the woman was altered by years, and ornaments, and dress, he thought that he had now recognized the face he had once seen by the lantern light. He felt excited at this discovery. He had numerous questions to ask. He brought together his palms and saluted her respectfully. He expected she would stop and speak to him. But she merely threw him an indifferent glance and passed on. He stood staring after her for a moment, baffled. 'Probably this is someone else,' he muttered and turned to go home, resolving to dismiss the whole episode from his mind.

Glossary

tank bund – dam
obstinate – stubborn
rupee – Indian currency
sole – only
ancestral – belonging to ancestors
kinsmen – relatives
privation – lack of everything needed for human well-being, e.g. food and warmth
bewilderment – amazement
staff – walking stick

Read the sentences a to h. Each sentence describes part of the **plot**, but they are in the wrong order. Sort them into the right order.

a The watchman feels responsible for the girl's apparent suicide.
b The watchman is reminded of his own troubles and tragedies in life.
c The girl ignores the watchman and walks by him without speaking.
d The watchman sees the girl again years later.
e The watchman loses sympathy with the girl, and tells her to go home.
f The watchman gets ready to leave for home, when he sees a figure.
g The girl tells the watchman she has no home in this world.
h The girl explains she has not got a scholarship, and will have to marry.

Password →

Plot

A **plot** is what happens in the story. It usually has a basic structure:

The **opening** – which grabs the reader's attention so they want to know more
The **complication** – where the main problem/task is revealed
The **crisis** – where the problem/task comes to a head, often dramatically
The **resolution** – where the problem is solved, and the ending can be reached.

 Think about the society described in this story. Is it different from your own society? Which clues tell you that this story may come from a different **culture** to the one you are used to?

Password →

Culture

The traditions, arts, achievements, and society of a particular country are often referred to as its **culture**. Cultures vary a lot from country to country.

3 The first paragraph of a story can give the reader clues about what will happen later on. Reread the first paragraph of this story.

a) Why is it important that it is dark and quiet?
b) How does the fisherman's mood and behaviour match the mood of the story?
c) Pick out the key words that are used to describe him.

4 The characters of the watchman and the girl are very different. They come from different backgrounds and have completely different expectations of life.

Copy and complete the table below. Look carefully at what the girl says about her family, and also how the characters act in the final paragraph of the story.

The watchman	The girl
Grew up as an orphan	
Is fairly old – 65	
Has little money – 20 rupees is a month's wages to him	
Lost his parents, siblings and most of his children	
Works as a watchman until late in the day	
Seems only to wish for a quiet life	

5 At the beginning of the story, how does the watchman react:

a) when he first realizes that a person is getting into the water?
b) when the girl tells him why she is unhappy?

6 Towards the end of the story, we find out that the watchman's feelings changed overnight.

a) What does he think happened to the girl?
b) How does he feel about the dam?
Use quotations from the text as evidence.

7 In pairs or a small group, discuss the girl's feelings towards the watchman at each stage of the story.

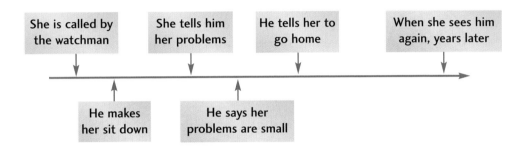

| She is called by the watchman | She tells him her problems | He tells her to go home | When she sees him again, years later |

| He makes her sit down | He says her problems are small |

 8 Use the **PEE structure** to write a paragraph about what you think happens at the end of the story. Many answers are possible, but remember to back up your ideas with evidence from the story.

Password →

PEE structure

PEE stands for Point, Evidence, Explanation. It is a useful method to use when structuring a piece of writing.

For example:
  In the story, the young girl is upset. (POINT) We know this because her face is 'wet with tears'. (EVIDENCE) This makes the reader feel sorry for her and we ask ourselves what might be wrong. (EXPLANATION)

I feel troubled because...

I am sad because...

9 In pairs, take on the role of the watchman and the girl in their final meeting.

a) Make notes about how you think the characters feel.

b) Write a brief script of what they might say to each other, or improvise a conversation they might have.

Round-up

With a partner, list:

► what sorts of things in a text tell you it is from a specific culture
► the ways that writers express emotion in a text.

Over to you

Using the work you have done in this unit so far, answer the following question.

Explain how the watchman's emotions change through the story in relation to:

► the girl
► the tank (reservoir)
► his own life.

→ Remember!

Think carefully about:
► the characters and the way they are revealed to the reader
► setting
► language
► the passage of time
► using the PEE structure.

Plan

Use a mind map like the one on the next page to jot down your ideas for each bullet point in the question.

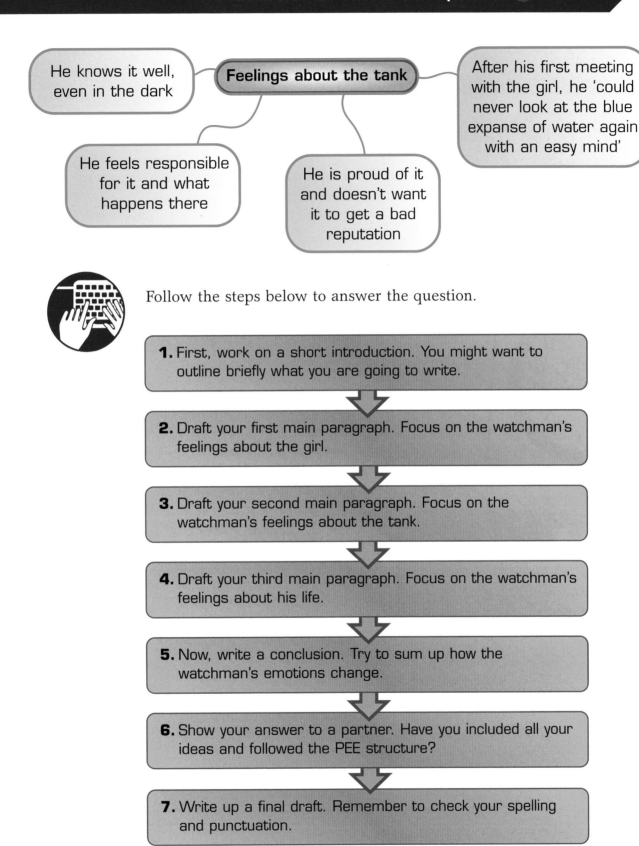

He knows it well, even in the dark

Feelings about the tank

After his first meeting with the girl, he 'could never look at the blue expanse of water again with an easy mind'

He feels responsible for it and what happens there

He is proud of it and doesn't want it to get a bad reputation

Follow the steps below to answer the question.

1. First, work on a short introduction. You might want to outline briefly what you are going to write.

2. Draft your first main paragraph. Focus on the watchman's feelings about the girl.

3. Draft your second main paragraph. Focus on the watchman's feelings about the tank.

4. Draft your third main paragraph. Focus on the watchman's feelings about his life.

5. Now, write a conclusion. Try to sum up how the watchman's emotions change.

6. Show your answer to a partner. Have you included all your ideas and followed the PEE structure?

7. Write up a final draft. Remember to check your spelling and punctuation.

1984

George Orwell's classic novel *1984* was first published in 1949. At that time, the story was a vision of the future. Orwell describes a society that is watched and controlled by Big Brother. His vision of the future is like a nightmare.

Read Orwell's opening.

1 It was a bright cold day in April, and the clocks were striking thirteen. Winston Smith, his chin nuzzled into his breast in an effort to escape the vile wind, slipped quickly through the glass doors of Victory Mansions, though not quickly enough to prevent a swirl of gritty dust from entering along with him.

2 The hallway smelt of boiled cabbage and old rag mats. At one end of it a coloured poster, too large for indoor display, had been tacked to the wall. It depicted simply an enormous face, more than a metre wide: the face of a man of about forty-five, with a heavy black moustache and ruggedly handsome features. Winston made for the stairs. It was no use trying the lift. Even at the best of times it was seldom working, and at present the electric current was cut off during daylight hours. It was part of the economy drive in preparation for Hate Week. The flat was seven flights up, and Winston, who was thirty-nine and had a varicose ulcer above his right ankle, went slowly, resting several times on the way. On each landing, opposite the lift shaft, the poster with the enormous face gazed from the wall. It was one of those pictures which are so contrived that the eyes follow you about when you move. BIG BROTHER IS WATCHING YOU, the caption beneath it ran.

Glossary
depicted – showed
ruggedly – rough and strong
varicose ulcer – a swollen, open sore
contrived – created

1 From the very first sentence, the reader knows that the world being described is not like the world we live in. Which one word tells us this?

2 The extract is taken from a very powerful story. In pairs, or a small group, discuss the emotions you felt when reading the extract. Record them on a spider diagram like the one on page 15.

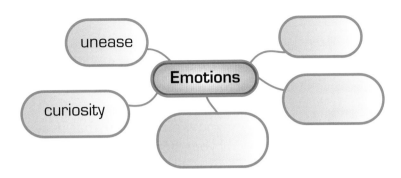

3 George Orwell makes the reader feel the physical discomfort of the scene. He does this by describing what Winston feels, through his senses. Copy and complete the grid below.

Sense	Phrase
Sight	
Sound	
Smell/Taste	
Touch	'swirl of gritty dust'

4 Orwell is an expert at using just one word to suggest a lot of things to the reader. In the extract, for example, Winston Smith enters a building called 'Victory Mansions'.

a) What does the word 'victory' make you think about? Start your answer like this:

The use of the word 'Victory' for the name of the building suggests that ...

b) Orwell uses **irony** in this description. How is the meaning of 'victory' different from the way the rest of the extract makes you feel?

Password →

Irony

Irony is when we express ourselves using language that usually means the opposite.

For example, if you are going on a picnic and it starts to rain, someone might say 'Great weather for a picnic!'

5 A large poster is described in the extract. In pairs, or a small group, discuss what you think this poster might look like. Talk about the colours, the shape of the eyes, etc.

6 Imagine how you would feel if that poster covered one wall in every room of your house – including your bedroom. Would it make you act in a different way?

7 What do we find out about Winston Smith in the extract? Think about his state of mind as well as his physical health.

Round-up

With a partner, discuss what you have learnt about:

- ➤ how sensory description can make the story feel real to the reader
- ➤ how just a few powerful words and phrases can build up powerful images and atmosphere.

Share your ideas with another pair or the rest of the class.

Over to you

In an exam, you might be asked a question about the themes in a narrative. Answer the following question about the opening of *1984*. Aim to write one paragraph about each bullet point.

Show how Orwell expresses a feeling of negativity through the following:

- ➤ the description of place
- ➤ the description of society
- ➤ the use of character

> ### → Remember!
> Think carefully about:
> ➤ the use of language and individual words
> ➤ the meanings behind words
> ➤ how themes are revealed
> ➤ emotive language
> ➤ using the PEE structure.

Use a mind map to jot down your ideas for each bullet point in the question.

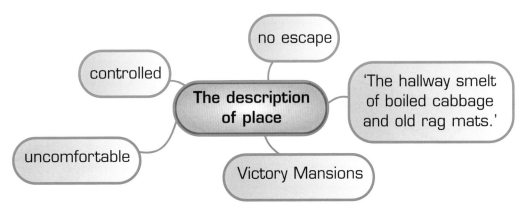

 Follow the steps below to answer the question.

1. Draft an introductory paragraph.

2. In your first main paragraph, tackle the description of place.

3. In your second main paragraph, focus on the description of society.

4. In your third main paragraph, focus on the use of character.

5. In your conclusion, try to sum up your feelings about the text.

Narratives: structure

In this unit you will:

➤ look at a variety of narratives
➤ explore different ways to structure a narrative
➤ experiment with different ways of opening,
  developing and ending paragraphs
➤ work on a narrative of your own.

Get started

As a reader, what do you think makes a story successful? Is it the characters, the plot, the setting, the tension, humour, element of surprise, etc? With a partner, talk about some of your favourite stories (they could be in books, films or TV dramas) and why you think they are successful. Jot down your ideas.

In this unit, you are going to focus on how to write a successful story.

Planning narratives

At the core of every story is a **plot**. The first thing to think about when writing a story is how the plot will unfold.

Password →

Plot

A **plot** is what happens in the story. It usually has a basic structure:

The **opening** – which grabs the reader's attention so they want to know more

The **complication** – where the main problem/task is revealed

The **crisis** – where the problem/task comes to a head, often dramatically

The **resolution** – where the problem is solved, and the ending can be reached.

1 Imagine you are writing a story about a downtrodden American Football team that needs to win a game to save the club from bankruptcy.

Look at the simple plot plan below. Its stages have got mixed up. Put them into the correct order.

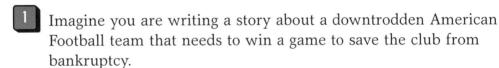

a At half time, at level scores, their lead quarterback is knocked out and can't play.

b The youngest reserve quarterback has to make the final vital play.

c The team win the final play, win the game and save the club.

d The opening play goes badly wrong, and they lose the ball.

e They comeback with three amazing touchdowns.

f The opposing team score three times in a row.

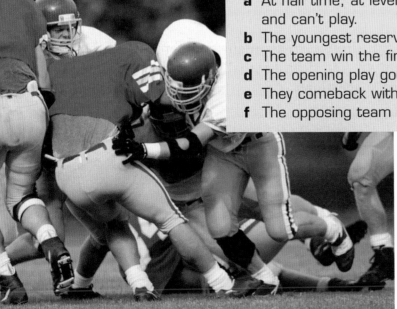

2 Which **genre** might a story about an American Football team belong to? How can you tell?

Password →

Genre

A **genre** is a type. Narratives of any kind can be sorted into different genres, e.g. adventure, crime, science fiction, historical, fantasy.

Some stories are a mix of genre, e.g. historical romance.

3 Now think about **audience**. Who might be interested in reading a sports story about an American Football team? In pairs, come up with two or three suggestions.

Password →

Audience

The **audience** is the people who read the text. In written texts the audience is often referred to as the 'reader' or 'readers'.

4 Copy and complete the table below. Brainstorm as many different audiences as you can for each genre. Think about interest groups as well as age groups. You can add other genres and their audiences too, if you wish.

Genre	Possible audiences
Science fiction	Teenagers, young adults, people interested in how the world might be in the future, and in scientific developments
Medical drama	Non-squeamish adults, some teenagers
Horror	Teenagers and young adults who enjoy being scared (or pretending they are not!)
War	
Fantasy	
Comedy	

Over to you

Now plan a narrative of your own.

1 Decide on your audience and genre.

2 Write a plot plan. Use the table below to help you.

Stage	Brief description
1 (Opening)	
2	
3	
4	
5	
6 (Ending)	

Narrative openings

1 Imagine you have picked up a book, opened it at the first page and started to read. After the first few paragraphs, you close the book and put it back on the shelf. What has happened?

a) The story is brilliant – really exciting – and makes you want to read on.
b) The story is deadly dull and boring.
c) It is a very short story.

(Choose one answer.)

The most important part of a story is its opening. If this is interesting and attention-grabbing, then the reader (or examiner!) will be impressed and want to read on.

2 Below are some jumbled up sentences about story openings. Sort them into two lists, headed DOs and DON'Ts.

Bore the reader with long explanations.

Introduce a situation or event that grips the reader with curiosity.

Start with 'Once upon a time' or 'A long time ago'.

Confuse the reader by introducing too many characters.

Build a sense of place so that the reader can imagine it in his or her mind.

Introduce the main character so that the reader is interested in his or her life.

3 Look at your DON'Ts list. Explain why it is important to avoid doing each of these things.

Read the opening from *The Fellowship of the Ring* on the next page. This is the first part in J.R.R. Tolkien's Middle Earth trilogy, *The Lord of the Rings*.

When Mr Bilbo Baggins of Bag End announced that he would shortly be celebrating his eleventy-first birthday with a party of special magnificence, there was much talk and excitement in Hobbiton.

Bilbo was very rich and very peculiar, and had been the wonder of the Shire for sixty years, ever since his remarkable disappearance and unexpected return. The riches he had brought back from his travels had now become a local legend, and it was popularly believed, whatever the old folk might say, that the hill at Bag End was full of tunnels stuffed with treasure. And if that was not enough for fame, there was also his prolonged vigour to wonder at. Time wore on, but it seemed to have little effect on Mr Baggins. At ninety he was much the same as at fifty. At ninety-nine they began to call him well-preserved, but unchanged would have been nearer the mark. There were some that shook their heads and thought this was too much of a good thing; it seemed unfair that anyone should possess (apparently) perpetual youth as well as (reputedly) inexhaustible wealth.

'It will have to be paid for,' they said. 'It isn't natural, and trouble will come of it!'

> **prolonged** – extended
> **vigour** – physical strength and good health
> **perpetual** – never-ending
> **reputedly** – reportedly
> **inexhaustible** – unable to be used up because there is so much of something

4 What are the three main **points of focus** in this opening?

Password →

Points of focus

A successful opening usually has three **points of focus**: character, place and action. It is usual to include all three, but to concentrate on one point focus more than the rest.

5 Which point of focus do you think is the strongest?

6 What is the first thing we discover about Mr Bilbo Baggins? Why is this interesting?

7 The table below shows some quotes from the text along with the reasons why they are interesting. Copy and complete the table. Add quotes and reasons of your own.

Quote	Why this is interesting
Bilbo 'had been the wonder of the Shire for sixty years'	If others are interested in him, we want to know why.
'his prolonged vigour'	Why is he living for so long?

8 The words Tolkien uses to describe Bilbo are particularly positive and impressive. In pairs, list the interesting words that describe Bilbo and his actions.

9 Now group the words you have listed into categories, e.g. 'unexpected', 'wonder' and 'magnificent' might be in the category 'exciting words'.

10 Read the sentence below. What **literary device** does the writer use to make the scene 'come alive' for his or her readers?

Creepers grew leisurely around the house, as old newspapers and carrier bags were tangled in the long weeds that strangled the gate.

 Password →

Literary devices

Writers use a variety of **literary devices** to make descriptions powerful.
➤ Similes ('as hot as a furnace') and metaphors ('the fields were covered in a beautiful white blanket') for comparison.
➤ Personification to give human qualities to objects or animals ('the leaves in the trees whispered quietly in the breeze').
➤ Assonance and alliteration to echo sound patterns.

11 Rewrite the sentence below to make the scene more descriptive and powerful. Use at least one literary device. Expand it into two sentences if you wish.

The girl walked down the road towards the cinema doors, which looked like they were locked.

Round-up

With a partner, list:
➤ three things to remember when planning a narrative
➤ three things to remember when writing an opening to a narrative.

Over to you

You are now going to write your own story opening, using what you have learnt in this unit so far.

Look back at your plot plan and think about the opening of your story. Try to picture the first scene in your head.

> **Remember!**
>
> Think carefully about:
> ➤ the genre
> ➤ the audience
> ➤ the main point of focus
> ➤ the language you will use to hook the reader
> ➤ the literary devices you will use to make your description interesting.

Plan

Use a mind map like the one below to jot down some of the details you want to include in your opening.

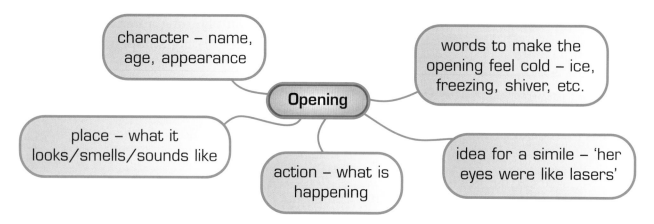

character – name, age, appearance

words to make the opening feel cold – ice, freezing, shiver, etc.

Opening

place – what it looks/smells/sounds like

action – what is happening

idea for a simile – 'her eyes were like lasers'

Follow the steps below to write your opening.

1. Choose your points of focus and decide which your main one is.

2. Write the opening sentence. Remember – this line needs to grab the reader's attention, so you could:
  ➤ include a detail that is surprising
  ➤ open at a dramatic moment of action
  ➤ open with emotional dialogue or speech.

3. Decide on how you can include description to get an idea or image across to the reader.

4. Choose some interesting words to include.

5. When you have finished your first draft, read it through or give it to a partner. Will it grab the reader's attention?

6. Make any changes to add interest to your opening.

Narrative endings

The ending of a story is as important as its beginning. If the ending is uninteresting or too easy to predict, the reader will not be impressed. On the other hand, if the ending is unexpected, exciting and powerful, the reader might wish there was more for them to read!

1 Below are some jumbled up sentences about story endings. Sort them into two lists, headed DOs and DON'Ts.

Introduce a new, important character at the last minute.

Tie up most loose ends.

Use expressive description to keep the reader hooked.

Explain the story away by saying it was a dream or an alien abduction.

Include a comment from or about the main character.

Be really obvious.

2 Look at your DON'Ts list. Explain why it is not a good idea to do these things when ending a story.

In the story of *Dr Jekyll and Mr Hyde* by Robert Louis Stevenson, Dr Jekyll invents a potion that turns him from a kind, handsome gentleman into a terrible, murderous beast – Mr Hyde. After some time, Jekyll decides he doesn't want to turn into Hyde any more, but it is too late. Jekyll has been taken over by Hyde and he can't turn himself back. When Hyde kills himself, Jekyll dies with him.

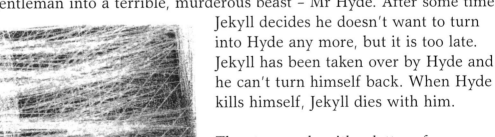

The story ends with a letter of confession Jekyll leaves for a friend to read after his death.

About a week passed, and I am now finishing this statement under the influence of the last of the old powders. This, then, is the last time, short of a miracle, that Henry Jekyll can think his own thoughts or see his own face (now how sadly altered!) in the glass. Nor must I delay too long to bring my writing to an end; for if my narrative has hitherto escaped destruction, it has been by a combination of great prudence and great good luck. Should the throes of change take me in the act of writing it, Hyde will tear it in pieces; but if some time shall have elapsed after I have laid it by, his wonderful selfishness and circumscription to the moment will probably save it once again from the action of his ape-like spite. And indeed the doom that is closing in on us both has already changed and crushed him. Half an hour from now, when I shall again and for ever reindue that hated personality, I know how I shall sit shuddering and weeping in my chair, or continue, with the most strained and fearstruck ecstasy of listening, to pace up and down this room (my last earthly refuge) and give ear to every sound of menace. Will Hyde die upon the scaffold? or will he find the courage to release himself at the last moment? God knows; I am careless; this is my true hour of death, and what is to follow concerns another than myself. Here, then, as I lay down the pen, and proceed to seal up my confession, I bring the life of that unhappy Henry Jekyll to an end.

Glossary
powders – potions
hitherto – so far
prudence – care
throes – intense, violent struggles
elapsed – passed
circumscription - restriction
reindue – become
refuge – shelter
menace – threat

Wish you were here!
Love,
Katy
P.S.

3 Think about the main point of focus in this ending. Is it character, place or action?

4 Which words show Jekyll's fear and hatred of Hyde?

5 Stevenson builds suspense when he asks:

'Will Hyde die upon the scaffold? or will he find the courage to release himself at the last moment?'

What does this mean?

One of the reasons this ending is so effective is that the story is not quite tied up – we are not told what happens to Hyde after Jekyll 'dies'. In pairs, or a small group, discuss what you think might happen to the character of Hyde. Together, write a few sentences as a **postscript** to the story.

 Password ➔

Postscripts

A **postscript** is a section attached to the end of a text, which can include extra or concluding information. Postscripts can appear at the end of narratives and letters and often begin with the short form 'PS'.

Round-up

With a partner, list three things to remember when writing the ending to a narrative.

Over to you

You are now going to write the ending to your story. Look back at your plan and story opening. Now try to picture the final scene in your head.

➔ **Remember!**

Think carefully about:
➤ genre and audience
➤ the expressive description you will use to keep the reader hooked
➤ how you will tie up loose ends or leave your reader to wonder
➤ how you want the reader to feel – surprised? frightened? comforted? in suspense?

Plan

Use a mind map to jot down your ideas.

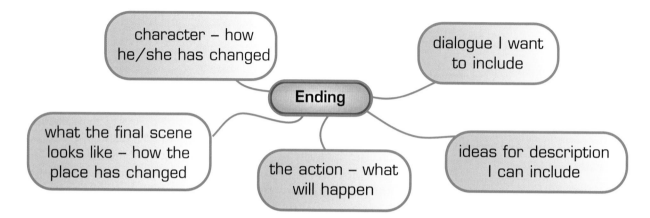

 Follow the steps below to write your ending.

1. Write a first draft.

2. Read through what you have written. Have you remembered everything?

3. Ask a partner for his or her opinion. Is your ending strong enough?

4. Make any final changes to your ending. Remember to check your spelling and punctuation.

In this unit you will:

➤ explore the meaning of several poems
➤ look at a variety of words poets choose and why
➤ investigate what poems tell us about the culture they are from
➤ write a poem.

Get started

Poets spend a lot of time crafting their poems. Each word is carefully selected to make the audience react in a certain way. The way a poem is laid out on the page – its 'form' – adds to its meaning, too.

In pairs, think about the poems you know. Try to remember the form of each one. Can you think of any poems where the form is especially important?

(Hint: think about limericks, haiku, etc.)

Exploring a poem

Read the following poem by Simon Armitage. If it helps you to feel the rhythm, read it aloud.

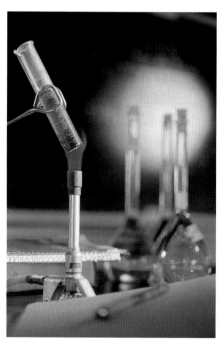

I Am Very Bothered

I am very bothered when I think
of the bad things that I have done in my life.
Not least that time in the chemistry lab
when I held a pair of scissors by the blades
5 and played the handles
in the naked lilac flame of the Bunsen burner;
then called your name, and handed them over.

O the unrivalled stench of branded skin
as you slipped your thumb and middle finger in,
10 then couldn't shake off the two burning rings. Marked,
the doctor said, for eternity.

Don't believe me, please, if I say
that was just my butterfingered way, at thirteen,
of asking you if you would marry me.

Glossary
unrivalled stench – a stronger smell than any other
branded – marked by burning

1. The character in the poem owns up to something he did at school. List the words in the poem that show he feels guilty.

2. With a partner, write a paragraph to explain exactly what the boy did. Include as much detail as you can, but keep your language simple.

3. The poem is divided into three sections. Each section has its own focus. Copy the lists on page 33. Match each section to its correct focus.

Section	Focus
1 (lines 1 – 7)	Gives a reason why he did it.
2 (lines 8 – 11)	Gives a brief outline of what he did.
3 (lines 12 – 14)	Explains the effect of what he did.

4 Look at the form of the poem. What type of poetic form does it remind you of? (Hint: count the total number of lines in the poem.)

5 How is this poem:

> ➤ similar to a traditional **sonnet**?
> ➤ different from a traditional sonnet?

Password →

Sonnets

All **sonnets** follow a set of rules, or conventions.

➤ They must have 14 lines.
➤ Shakespearean sonnets are split up into three sections, or quatrains. Each quatrain has four lines.
➤ Shakespearean sonnets usually follow the rhyme scheme *ababcdcdefefgg*.

6 Why do you think Armitage chose to use the sonnet form? (Hint: think about the usual theme of a traditional sonnet.)

7 Unlike many traditional sonnets, this sonnet does not have a regular rhythm or rhyme scheme. It does, however, have examples of internal **rhyme**.

How many examples of rhyme can you spot in the poem? Record your findings in a table like the one below.

Examples of internal rhyme in 'I Am Very Bothered'

Rhyme

Words **rhyme** when their end sounds match.

For example:
Hatch/thatch or cold/bold

Internal rhyme is when words in the same line rhyme.

For example:
   The n<u>ice</u> m<u>ice</u> liked sugar and sp<u>ice</u>.

Half rhyme is when words almost rhyme.

For example:
   Man/pun or relish/polish

 Pick out some examples of **alliteration** in the poem. Why do you think Armitage has used this poetic device?

Alliteration

Alliteration is when two or more words that are near each other begin with the same sound.

For example:
   It was <u>ch</u>illy as they stood outside the <u>ch</u>urch.

Often poets use alliteration to emphasize a sound. This can also help to reinforce a meaning.

 In 'I Am Very Bothered', what do you think Armitage is saying about young adults showing affection?

Looking at two poems

1 Look at the skeleton poems below. In pairs, discuss what you can say about the **form** of the poems just by looking at their skeletons.

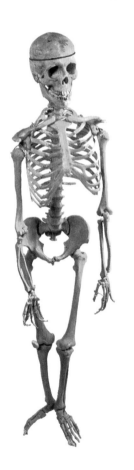

A

Xxxxxxxxxxx

Xxxx xxxxxx xxxxxxxx xxxx
Xxx xxxx xx xxx xxxxx,
Xx xxx xxxxxxx
Xxx xxxx xxxxx xxxx xxxx.

Xxxx xxxxxx xxxxxxxx xxxx,
Xxxx xxxx xxx xxx xx,
Xxx xxxxx x xxxxx xx xxx xxxxxx
Xxx xxxx xxxxx xxxx xxxxx.

Xxxxx xxxxxx xxxxxxxx xxxx,
Xxx xxxxx xxxx xxx xxx,
Xxx xxx xxxx xxxxxxxxxxx xxxx
Xxx xxxx xxxxx xxxx xxx.

Xxx xxxxxx xxxxxxxx xxxx,
Xxxxx xxx xxx xxxx,
Xxx xxx xx xxx xxxxxxxx xxxxx
Xxxx xxxxx xxx xxx.

Xxx xxxxxx xxxxxxxx xxx,
Xxxx xxx xxxx xxx xxx,
Xxxxxx xxxx xxxx xxxxx xxxx
Xxxx xxxxx xxxx xxxx.

B

Xxxx Xxxxx

Xxxxxx xx
xxxxxxxx xx xxx xxx
X'x xxxx-xxxxx

Xxxxxxx xxxxxx
xxx xx xxxx
xxxx xx xxx xxxx-xxxxx
xx xxxx xxxx xxxxxxx
xxx xxx xx xxxxx
xx xx xxxx-xxxxx xxxxx
xxxxxxx xxxxxx
xxx xx xxxx
xxxx xx xxx xxxx-xxxxx
xx xxxx xxxx xxxxx xx xxxxxx
xxx xx xx xxx
xx x xxxx-xxxxx xxxxxxx
xxxx xx xxx xxxx
xxxxxxx xxxxxxx
xxxxxx xxxxxx xxxx-xxxxx
xx xxxx xxxx x xxx xxxxx
xxxx-xxxxx xxxx xxx xxxxxxxx
xx xxxxxxxx xxx xxxx xxxx xx xxx xxxx
xx xxxx
xxxxxxx xxxxxx
xxx xx xxxx
xxxx xx xxx xxxx-xxxxx
xx xxxx xxxxxxxxxxx
xxx xxxx xx xxx xxxxx
xx xxx x xxxxx xxx
xx x xxxx-xxxxx xxxxxxx

Password →

Form

When we talk about **form**, we mean the way a poem is arranged.

For example:
➤ the shape it has on the page,
➤ the number of lines and their length,
➤ the number of stanzas
➤ repeated patterns in the shape, etc.

Now read this extract from 'Hooliganism' by Peter Kett.
(Hint: this matches skeleton poem A.)

HOOLIGANISM

Five little football fans
One fell on the floor,
He got crushed
And then there were four.

Four little football fans,
Just like you and me,
One threw a penny at the goalie
And then there were three.

Three little football fans,
The other team did boo,
But the fans outnumbered them
And then there were two.

Two little football fans,
After all was done,
One ran on the football pitch
Then there was one.

One little football fan,
Glad his team had won,
Argued with some other fans
Then there were none.

2 This poem has a clear theme. In pairs, decide what you think this theme is.

3 How does the extract follow this theme through?
(Hint: look at what each stanza describes.)

4 Look at the language 'Hooliganism' is written in. Has Kett used dialect or **Standard English**? Explain how you can tell.

 Password → **Standard English**

Standard English is the formal vocabulary and grammar that can be used by English speakers everywhere.

It does not use words from dialects that are used in particular areas or by particular groups of people. It can be found in most books, news reports, and documentaries.

Next, read an extract from 'Half Caste' by John Agard.
(Hint: this matches skeleton poem B.)

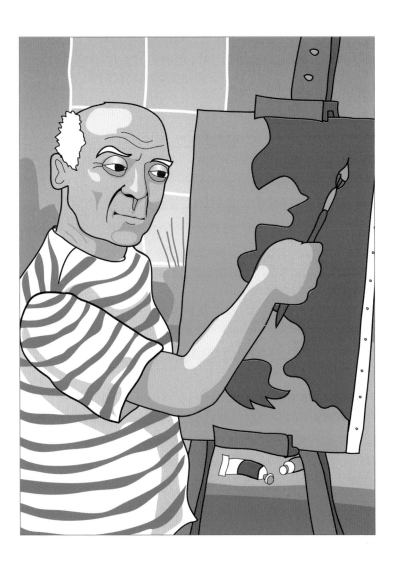

Half Caste

Excuse me
standing on one leg
I'm half-caste

Explain yuself
wha yu mean
when yu say half-caste
yu mean when picasso
mix red an green
is a half-caste canvas
explain yuself
wha yu mean
when yu say half-caste
yu mean when light an shadow
mix in de sky
is a half-caste weather
well in dat case
england weather
nearly always half-caste
in fact some o dem cloud
half-caste till dem overcast
so spiteful dem dont want de sun pass
ah rass
explain yuself
wha yu mean
when yu say half-caste
yu mean tchaikovsky
sit down at dah piano
an mix a black key
wid a white key
is a half-caste symphony
…

Glossary
yuself – yourself
wha – what
yu – you
an – and
mix – mixes/mixed
is – it's

de – the
dat – that
o – of
dem – them/they are/those/they
dah - the

ah rass – an expression of disgust
Tchaikovsky – a famous Russian composer of classical musical (born 1840, died 1893)

37

5 This poem has a clear theme. In pairs, decide what you think this theme is.

6 How does the extract follow this theme through? (Hint: look at what each section describes.)

7 In pairs, read 'Half Caste' again, this time aloud. Try to say each word exactly as it is written on the page. Is this poem written in Standard English like 'Hooliganism'?

8 'Half Caste' is written in dialect. Why do you think the poet has written in this kind of English?

 Password →

Dialect

A **dialect** is a form of a language that is peculiar to a specific region. It is not just about accent (the way words are pronounced). It can involve vocabulary and even sentence structure that is completely different to the standard form of the language.

---

9 Make a list of dialect words in the poem? (Hint: look at the glossary!)

10 Choose a few lines of the extract from 'Half Caste', then write them out in Standard English. Compare your new version with the original. Does the meaning change in the Standard English version?

11 The poet wants the reader to understand that using the term 'half caste' is a little silly and also quite rude. To make this clear, he uses a number of **metaphors**. List the metaphors can you find in the poem.

 Password →

Metaphors

A **metaphor** describes something as if it were something else.

For example: He is the king of skateboarding.

Comparing two poems

1 Look back at the extracts from 'Hooliganism' and 'Half Caste' on pages 36 and 37. Which did you feel was the easiest to understand? Why?

2 In 'Half Caste', John Agard uses humour to stress his serious message about language. Find some examples.

3 Do you think there are any humorous/serious sections in 'Hooliganism'? Explain your answer to a partner, then share your ideas with the class.

4 Think back to the skeleton versions of these two poems on page 35. Do you think form can help a poem to sound humorous/serious? Explain your ideas.

5 Both poems use **repetition**. Draw up, and complete, a table like the one started below.

Poem	Repeated word/phrase	Reason for repetition

Password → **Repetition**

Repetition is when certain words/phrases are repeated in a line, stanza or in the poem as a whole.

Poets take great care to write their poetry in a certain way, so if repetition is used it is usually important (not just an accident).

Round-up

With a partner, discuss how the following can make a difference to a poem:

➤ form
➤ theme
➤ language.

Over to you

The poems in this unit deal with topics and themes that the poets feel strongly about:

➤ In 'I Am Very Bothered', the topic is feelings of guilt and young love.
➤ In 'Hooliganism', the issue is how football hooligans ruin the sport of football.
➤ In 'Half Caste', the main theme is English terms and the way people use them incorrectly.

You are going to write a poem about a theme or issue you feel strongly about. It could be one of the following:

➤ Pocket money
➤ Using mobile phones in school
➤ Young people spending too long on computers
➤ Media focus on celebrities

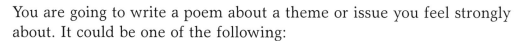

→ Remember!

Your poem may include some, or all, of the following:
➤ stanzas
➤ dialect words or expressions
➤ a form that follows or echoes a traditional pattern
➤ a clear rhyming pattern (end rhymes and internal rhymes)
➤ repetition of words/phrases for effect
➤ alliteration to emphasize a point or feeling
➤ similes and/or metaphors.

Plan

Use a mind map like the one below to jot down some ideas. This example is for a poem about pocket money.

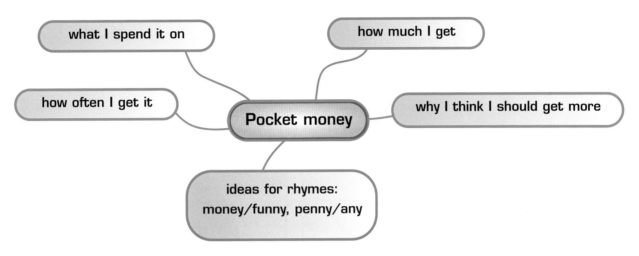

what I spend it on

how much I get

how often I get it

Pocket money

why I think I should get more

ideas for rhymes:
money/funny, penny/any

Now follow these steps to write your poem.

1. Decide on the form or shape your poem is going to take.

2. Make a note of any techniques you want to use (refer to the Remember panel).

3. Next, put the ideas from your mind map into an order.

4. Begin to draft your poem. At first, just try to get your thoughts down, roughly in the form you have chosen.

5. Read your first draft and show it to a partner. Can he or she suggest improvements?

6. Make any changes to your poem that you think would improve it. Check that each word is in the best possible position.

In this unit you will:

➤ learn how to analyse scenes from Shakespeare
➤ practise using quotations effectively
➤ produce a formal essay.

LADY MACBETH, WOULD YOU AT LEAST TRY AND LOOK DOMINATING?

... AND THERE ARE *NO* VOLCANOS IN SCOTLAND!

Get started

You may already be familiar with some of Shakespeare's plays. You might even have started focusing on one play in particular.

Being able to analyse scenes from a Shakespeare play is an important skill. You need to be able to write about Shakespeare's characters, language and themes. You also need to learn how to think like a director and imagine you are directing the scenes. There are many Shakespeare plays to choose from, but in this unit you will look at two scenes from *Macbeth*.

One of the key topics in *Macbeth* is the theme of temptation (when you really want to do something – especially something you know is wrong) and persuasion. With a partner, improvise a short scene to show:

> ➤ temptation (e.g. stealing from your mum's purse – you know it is wrong, but you really want to)
> ➤ persuasion (e.g. persuading a friend to do something he or she really does not want to do).

Examining a scene (1)

The first scene from *Macbeth* you are going to examine is Act 1, Scene 7.

Duncan is king of Scotland and his troops have recently won a battle. On their way home from the fighting, two of his men meet three witches. They tell one of the men – Macbeth – that he will one day be king. Macbeth likes this idea and realises that if he kills Duncan, then he will not have to wait so long to become king. However, he also feels a sense of duty towards Duncan because he is his king.

In this scene, Macbeth is having doubts about killing King Duncan, who is now a guest at his house. Lady Macbeth – who is hungry for power and dominates her husband – persuades him to change his mind.

Inside Macbeth's *castle. Hautboys. Torches.*
Enter a Sewer, *and divers* Servants *with dishes*
and service over the stage. Then enter Macbeth

Macbeth
If it were done when 'tis done, then 'twere well
It were done quickly. If th'assassination
Could trammel up the consequence and catch
With his surcease, success, that but this blow
5 Might be the be-all and the end-all—here,
But here, upon this bank and shoal of time,
We'd jump the life to come. But in these cases,
We still have judgement here that we but teach
10 Bloody instructions, which being taught, return
To plague th'inventor. This even-handed justice
Commends th'ingredients of our poison'd chalice
To our own lips. He's here in double trust:
First, as I am his kinsman and his subject,
15 Strong both against the deed; then, as his host,
Who should against his murderer shut the door,
Not bear the knife myself. Besides, this Duncan
Hath borne his faculties so meek, hath been
So clear in his great office, that his virtues
20 Will plead like angels, trumpet-tongu'd against
The deep damnation of his taking-off.
And pity, like a naked new-born babe
Striding the blast, or heaven's cherubin hors'd
Upon the sightless couriers of the air,
25 Shall blow the horrid deed in every eye,
That tears shall drown the wind. I have no spur
To prick the sides of my intent, but only
Vaulting ambition which o'erleaps itself
And falls on th'other—

Enter Lady Macbeth

How now? What news?

Lady Macbeth
He has almost supp'd. Why have you left the
chamber?

Macbeth
30 Hath he ask'd for me?

Lady Macbeth
Know you not he has?

Macbeth
We will proceed no further in this business.
He hath honour'd me of late, and I have bought
Golden opinions from all sorts of people,
Which would be worn now in their newest gloss,
35 Not cast aside so soon.

Lady Macbeth
Was the hope drunk
Wherein you dress'd yourself? Hath it slept since?
And wakes it now to look so green and pale
At what it did so freely? From this time,
Such I account thy love. Art thou afeard
40 To be the same in thine own act and valour,
As thou art in desire? Wouldst thou have that
Which thou esteem'st the ornament of life,
And live a coward in thine own esteem,
Letting 'I dare not' wait upon 'I would',
45 Like the poor cat i'th'adage?

Macbeth

Prithee, peace.
I dare do all that may become a man;
Who dares do more is none.

Lady Macbeth

What beast was't, then,
That made you break this enterprise to me?
When you durst do it, then you were a man.
50 And to be more than what you were, you would
Be so much more the man. Nor time, nor place
Did then adhere, and yet you would make both.
They have made themselves and that their fitness
    now
Does unmake you. I have given suck and know
55 How tender 'tis to love the babe that milks me:
I would, while it was smiling in my face,
Have pluck'd my nipple from his boneless gums,
And dash'd the brains out, had I so sworn
As you have done to this.

Macbeth

If we should fail?

Lady Macbeth

We fail?
60 But screw your courage to the sticking-place,
And we'll not fail. When Duncan is asleep,
Whereto the rather shall his day's hard journey
Soundly invite him, his two chamberlains
Will I with wine and wassail so convince

65 That memory, the warder of the brain,
Shall be a fume, and the receipt of reason
A limbeck only. When in swinish sleep
Their drenched natures lie as in a death,
What cannot you and I perform upon
70 Th'unguarded Duncan? What not put upon
His spongy officers, who shall bear the guilt
Of our great quell?

Macbeth

Bring forth men-children only,
For thy undaunted mettle should compose
Nothing but males. Will it not be receiv'd,
75 When we have mark'd with blood those sleepy
    two
Of his own chamber, and us'd their very daggers,
That they have done't?

Lady Macbeth

Who dares receive it other,
As we shall make our griefs and clamour roar
Upon his death?

Macbeth

I am settled and bend up
80 Each corporal agent to this terrible feat.
Away, and mock the time with fairest show,
False face must hide what the false heart doth
    know.

Exeunt

Glossary

Sewer – butler

trammel up (l.3) – prevent

surcease (l.4) – death

shoal (l.6) – shallow water

jump (l.7) – risk; leap over

Commends (l.11) – recommends

ingredience (l.11) – mixture of ingredients

chalice (l.11) – ceremonial cup

faculties (l.17) – powers

taking-off (l.20) – murder

bought (l.32) – earned

adage (l.45) – proverb

become (l.46) – be suitable for

break (l.48) – mention

adhere (l.52) – agree

limbeck (l.67) – an alchemist's distilling flask

put (l.70) – blame

quell (l.72) – kill

mettle (l.73) – courage

receiv'd (l.74) – believed

very (l.76) – own

settled (l.79) – decided

bend up (l.79) – brace

corporal agent (l.80) – physical faculty

mock (l.81) – deceive

1 The panels below describe what happens in the scene, but they are muddled up. Put them in the correct order. The first one is in the correct place.

a Macbeth is trying to decide whether or not to kill King Duncan: he is worried that if he does kill the king he will not be able to escape justice; he also knows that Duncan is a good man who trusts him.

b Macbeth decides to go ahead with the murder, but he knows that he will have to be two-faced from now on, and pretend that he is innocent.

c Lady Macbeth answers that they cannot fail if they have courage, and goes on to explain how they will manage the murder.

d Lady Macbeth thinks Macbeth is a coward and tells him so.

e Macbeth is rather scared by his wife's enthusiasm, but he also admires it and is starting to come around to the idea again.

f Macbeth says that he will do anything a man should do, but that killing a king is too much.

g Macbeth is worried that the plan might go wrong and that they might fail.

h Lady Macbeth comes in, looking for Macbeth.

i Macbeth tells his wife that he has decided not to kill Duncan, especially because Duncan has recently made Macbeth the Thane of Cawdor.

j Lady Macbeth is cross and tries to persuade Macbeth to change his mind. She says that she would kill her own child if she had promised to do so, and as Macbeth has promised to kill Duncan, he should stick to his decision.

k Lady Macbeth tells Macbeth that no one will suspect them because they will pretend to be very upset when Duncan's body is found.

2 Act 1, Scene 7 starts with Macbeth's **soliloquy**. Why did Shakespeare write soliloquies?

Password →

Soliloquy

A **soliloquy** is a speech that reveals the inner thoughts and feelings of a character. They are often spoken when a character is alone onstage.

3 In his soliloquy, Macbeth gives these reasons (and others) why he should not kill the king:

➤ You don't kill your guests.
➤ You don't kill a good man.
➤ The killer will be killed – justice will be done.

Copy the reasons out, putting them in the order that Macbeth says them.

4 In his soliloquy, what one reason does Macbeth give for killing the king?

5 How would you describe Macbeth at the opening of this scene?

6 Look back at your answer to Question 4. Try to extend your answer, using the **PEE structure**.

Password →

PEE structure

PEE stands for Point, Evidence, Explanation. It is a useful method to use when structuring a piece of writing
➤ First, make a short **point**.
➤ Next, use a quotation as **evidence** to prove your point.
➤ Then, **explain** the quotation.

During this soliloquy, Macbeth seems uncertain whether to kill the king or not, e.g.

'then, as his host,
Who should against his murderer shut the door,
Not bear the knife myself.'

One of the reasons Macbeth states for not killing the king is that the king is his guest. As his host, Macbeth should protect the king not kill him.

7 Are the sentences in this soliloquy long or short? In pairs, discuss why you think Shakespeare has written them in this way.

8 Reread lines 48–59. How would you describe Lady Macbeth? Write a short paragraph using the PEE structure. Use the table below to help focus your ideas.

Point	(Think of some adjectives to describe Lady Macbeth at this point.)
Evidence	(Find a quote to back up your description.)
Explanation	(Explain your evidence – how does it back up your description?)

9 Who do you think has the most power in this scene? How can you tell?

10 Shakespeare shows Lady Macbeth's power through her language. She uses many questions and commands when talking to her husband.

Write down one question and one **command** that she uses.

Password →

Commands

A **command** is a type of sentence. We use it when we want somebody to do something.

For example,
 Sit down!

Commands use the imperative form of a verb.

11 Imagine you are the **director** for a theatre production of *Macbeth*. How would you make the characters act in this scene?
(Hint: think about where the actors will stand. Will they be talking loudly? Will both characters sound the same? You might find it useful to act the scene out with a partner first.)

Password →

Director

The director of a play is the person who is in charge of making decisions about how the play will be acted and produced.

 Summarize your thoughts on Act 1, Scene 7. Copy and complete the table on page 50. Place the following key words in the correct column.

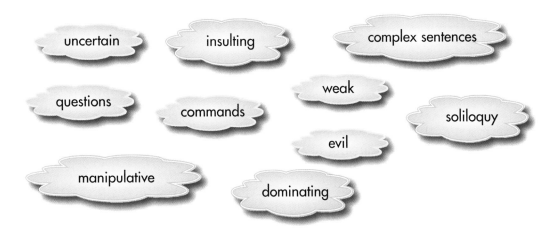

uncertain   insulting   complex sentences   questions   weak   commands   soliloquy   evil   manipulative   dominating

Lady Macbeth	Macbeth

13 Using the work you did for Question 12, write a short paragraph where you discuss the characters of Macbeth and Lady Macbeth in Act 1, Scene 7.

Examining a scene (2)

The next scene from *Macbeth* you are going to examine is Act 5, Scene 3.

Macbeth has killed King Duncan and is now king of Scotland himself. However, Macbeth is not happy with his new situation. He is haunted by the murders (of Duncan and others) he has committed. Also, Duncan's son – Malcolm – has teamed up with the English and is planning to meet Macbeth in battle for the crown.

Before you read Act 5, Scene 3, look at the sentences below. They describe what happens in the scene, but they are muddled up. See if you can work out the correct order. (This is just a first attempt. You can try again once you have read the scene.)

a | Macbeth is very angry with the servant for bringing the news.

b | Macbeth reminds himself of what the witches have said. He is sure that it is impossible for a wood to move, and just as sure that Malcolm was born of a woman and so cannot hurt him.

c | A servant enters and tells Macbeth that ten thousand soldiers are approaching.

d | The doctor says only Lady Macbeth can cure herself.

e | The doctor says Lady Macbeth is mentally ill.

f | The scene opens with Macbeth's announcement that he wants no more news about Malcolm's army.

g | Macbeth decides that this battle will either make or break him, and feels ready to die if necessary.

h | Macbeth is determined to fight to the death.

i | One of Macbeth's officers, Seyton, tells Macbeth that the servant's report is correct.

j | Macbeth declares he will not be afraid of death unless Birnam Wood moves to Dunsinane.

k | Macbeth asks the doctor if he can cure Lady Macbeth of her mental illness.

l | The doctor ends the scene by telling the audience that if he could get away from Dunsinane, he would stay away. This hints at bad things to come.

m | Macbeth calls again for his armour and tells the doctor to do what he can for Lady Macbeth.

n | Macbeth calls for his armour, then asks the doctor about Lady Macbeth.

In this scene, Macbeth receives the news that some of his soldiers are deserting him. He knows that this battle with Malcolm will make or break him, and he is determined to fight to the end. He calms himself by remembering what the witches have told him: first, that no man born of a woman can harm him; second, that he cannot be harmed until Birnam Wood (a nearby forest) moves to Dunsinane (Macbeth's castle). Macbeth knows that both of these things are impossible – all men are born of women and trees cannot move. We also learn that Lady Macbeth is suffering from a mental illness that cannot be cured. Her guilty feelings are killing her.

Dunsinane, Macbeth's *castle*: *enter* Macbeth, Doctor, *and* Attendants

Macbeth
Bring me no more reports, let them fly all;
Till Birnam wood remove to Dunsinane,
I cannot taint with fear. What's the boy Malcolm?
Was he not born of woman? The spirits that know
5 All mortal consequences have pronounc'd me
    thus:
'Fear not, Macbeth, no man that's born of woman
Shall e'er have power upon thee.' Then fly false
    thanes
And mingle with the English epicures;
The mind I sway by and the heart I bear
10 Shall never sag with doubt nor shake with fear.

Enter Servant

The devil damn thee black, thou cream-fac'd loon.
Where got'st thou that goose-look?

Servant
There is ten thousand—

Macbeth
                    Geese, villain?

Servant
                    Soldiers, sir.

Macbeth
Go prick thy face, and over-red thy fear,
15 Thou lily-liver'd boy. What soldiers, patch?
Death of thy soul, those linen cheeks of thine
Are counsellors to fear. What soldiers, whey-face?

Servant
The English force, so please you.

Macbeth
Take thy face hence!

Exit Servant

                    Seyton!—I am sick at heart,
20 When I behold—Seyton, I say! —this push
Will cheer me ever or disseat me now.
I have liv'd long enough. My way of life
Is fall'n into the sere, the yellow leaf;
And that which should accompany old age,
25 As honour, love, obedience, troops of friends,
I must not look to have; but, in their stead,

Curses, not loud but deep, mouth-honour, breath
Which the poor heart would fain deny, and dare
    not.

Seyton!

Enter Seyton

Seyton
30 What's your gracious pleasure?

Macbeth
                        What news more?

Seyton
All is confirm'd, my lord, which was reported.

Macbeth
I'll fight till from my bones my flesh be hack'd.
Give me my armour.

Seyton
'Tis not needed yet.

Macbeth
35 I'll put it on;
Send out more horses; skirr the country round.
Hang those that talk of fear. Give me mine
    armour.
How does your patient, doctor?

Doctor
                    Not so sick, my lord,
As she is troubled with thick-coming fancies

That keep her from her rest.

Macbeth
                        Cure her of that.
Canst thou not minister to a mind diseas'd,
Pluck from the memory a rooted sorrow,
Raze out the written troubles of the brain,
And with some sweet oblivious antidote
45 Cleanse the stuff'd bosom of that perilous stuff
Which weighs upon the heart?

Doctor
                        Therein the patient
Must minister to himself.

Macbeth
Throw physic to the dogs, I'll none of it.
Come, put mine armour on; give me my staff.—
50 Seyton, send out.— Doctor, the thanes fly from
    me.—
[*To* Attendant] Come, sir, dispatch.— If thou
    couldst, doctor, cast
The water of my land, find her disease,
And purge it to a sound and pristine health,
I would applaud thee to the very echo
55 That should applaud again.—Pull't off, I say!—
What rhubarb, cynne, or what purgative drug
Would scour these English hence? Hear'st thou
    of them?

Doctor
Ay, my good lord; your royal preparation
Makes us hear something.

Macbeth
                        Bring it after me.—
60 I will not be afraid of death and bane,
Till Birnam Forest come to Dunsinane.

Exeunt all but Doctor

Doctor
Were I from Dunsinane away and clear,
Profit again should hardly draw me here.

Exit

Glossary

taint (l.3) – lose courage

mortal consequences (l.5) – human fates

pronounc'd (l.5) – told

e'er (l.7) – ever

the English epicures (l.8) – the soft-living English

sway (l.9) – rule myself

cream-fac'd (l.11) – white-faced

loon (l.11) – villain

over-red (l.14) – paint red over

lily-liver'd (l.15) – cowardly

patch (l.15) – idiot

whey-face (l.17) – milk-face

push (l.20) – attack

disseat (l.21) – de-throne

sere (l.23) – dry, withered

mouth-honour (l.27) – flattery

fain (l.28) – willingly

skirr (l.36) – scour, search

thick-coming (l.39) – coming in quick succession

fancies (l.39) – imaginings

minister to (l.41) – treat

oblivious (l.44) – causing forgetfulness

stuff'd bosom (l.45) – burdened heart

physic (l.48) – medicine

dispatch (l.51) – hurry up

rhubarb, cynne (l.56) – medicinal plants

scour (l.57) – drive out

bane (l.60) - destruction

---

1 At this point in the play, Lady Macbeth is very different to how she was in Act 1, Scene 7. Using the PEE structure, write a paragraph to show how Lady Macbeth has changed.

2 In lines 13–18, a soldier tells Macbeth that Malcolm's army is near. How does Macbeth react?

3 What could Macbeth's reaction to the soldier's news show about his state of mind?

4 Macbeth seems ruthless about killing now. Find an example of how he is not afraid to order the killing of others.

5 Macbeth is determined to fight to the end. He says, 'I'll fight till from my bones my flesh be hack'd'. Describe the image this speech creates in your mind.

6 In pairs, think about which words you would now use to describe Macbeth? Make a list.

7 Macbeth's final speech in this scene is a **rhyming couplet**. Why do you think Shakespeare wrote it in this way?

Password →

Rhyming couplets

A **rhyming couplet** is the name for two lines of rhyming verse. They are often used to highlight something important or to signal the end of a scene or speech.

Round-up

In pairs, make a list of four things to remember when analysing a scene from Shakespeare e.g. pick out key words and phrases. Then share your ideas with the rest of the class.

Over to you

In an exam, you could find a question like the one below. Use the work you have done to answer this question on Act 1, Scene 7 and Act 5, Scene 3 of *Macbeth*.

How does the character of Macbeth change in these scenes?

→ Remember!

➤ Pick out key words and phrases.
➤ Look at the imagery in the speeches.
➤ Use the PEE structure in your answer.
➤ Think about how Macbeth talks to other characters.
➤ Think about Macbeth's actions.
➤ Think about Macbeth's feelings and emotions.

Use a planning grid like the one below to structure your ideas. Aim to write four or five paragraphs on each of the scenes.

First scene	Second scene
P E E	P E E
P E E	P E E

Now follow the steps below to answer the question.

1. First, work on your introduction. This should be no longer than one paragraph.
(Hint: say what you are going to discuss in your main paragraphs.)

2. Draft the first part of your answer. Focus on the first scene.

3. Draft the second part of your answer. Focus on the second scene and how the character has changed here.

4. Write a conclusion. Try to summarize your feelings about how the character has changed.

5. Share your work with a partner. Have you covered everything you wanted to cover? Check that you have used the PEE structure.

6. Write up your work. Remember to check your spelling and punctuation.

Media texts

In this unit you will:

- ➤ identify some of the key features of media texts
- ➤ think about the effect your writing, design and layout has on your audience
- ➤ take information from various sources and shape it into one media text
- ➤ design your own web page for a reality TV show.

Get started

In the world we live in today, the media is everywhere – in the shape of newspapers, magazines, television, radio, the Internet, plus in many less obvious ways. It is said that, from the moment you open your eyes to the moment you close them again at night, you could have over 1,500 messages aimed at you.

In this unit, you will focus on the skills you need to read and interpret two types of media text: a web page and an editorial.

With a partner, jot down some of the media messages that you have seen today.

Web sites

The media are always trying to get – and keep – our attention. For a few years now, many television companies have tried to bring their audiences something different. The result has been a range of reality TV shows.

1 In pairs, write down the names of as many different reality TV shows as you can think of in one minute.

2 Look at the page from a web site on page 59. Which reality TV show is this web site linked to?

3 Web sites can have a variety of purposes. What is the purpose of this site?

4 For all types of media text, presentation is very important. Designers work on the look and layout of a text to make it appealing and entertaining. In pairs, make a list of all the design features you recognize on this web page.
(Hint: for example, if the web site is sponsored, you will normally find the sponsor's **logo**.)

Password ➜

Logo

A **logo** is a design that a company or organization uses to identify its products. It is designed to be instantly recognizable, so that when someone sees it they know immediately who has made the product.

American Idol

MONDAY and TUESDAY 8/7c; WEDNESDAY 9/8c on FOX

HOME   CONTESTANTS   PHOTOS & VIDEO S   RECAP   EXCLUSIVES   COMMUNITY   SHOW INFO   NEWSLETTER

THE AMERICAN IDOL STORE

 THE OFFICIAL AMERICAN IDOL PHONE
GET MESSAGES FROM SIMON AND A CHANCE TO WIN A TRIP TO THE FINAL RESULTS SHOW *Tell me More!*

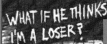 WHAT IF HE THINKS I'M A LOSER? WHAT R U AFRAID OF?

DIANA. FANTASIA. JASMINE. WHICH ONE WILL BECOME THE NEXT AMERICAN IDOL?

MONDAY SPECIAL PROGRAMME NOTE
Don't miss an all-new special featuring the final three Monday night at 8/7c on FOX. Ryan will sit down with the judges one on one to learn what they think about this season, and then Diana, Fantasia and Jasmine will sing one song each!

NEW IDOLONFOX.COM FEATURES LAUNCHED!

MY DRIVE WITH SIMON
Watch the exclusive interview with the man himself -- Simon Cowell -- as he drives to the Idol set. Get insight into his childhood, career, life and more…
Part 1 | Part 2 | Part 3 | Full Length Clip

Catch our **VIDEO EXCLUSIVES** from behind the scenes and also what happens during a **COUNTDOWN TO SHOWTIME** from the fans' point of view!

Try the **VIRTUAL SALON** where you get to style your favourite Idol's hair and hair color then send to a friend!

New **VIDEO CLIPS** and **PHOTOS** are being added every week. Be sure to check them out!

AMERICAN IDOL CALENDAR AND MOUSEPAD
Customize the products with American Idol pictures of your choice and personalize them with your own name and picture.
ORDER NOW !!

IDOL POLL

What kind of song will it take to win it all?
- Upbeat and fun
- An old classic
- Slow and sultry
- Something that rocks

ALL NEW PERFORMANCE CLIPS

IDOL TOUR TICKETS
American Idols live was one of the hottest tours last year and they're hitting the road again this summer for 2004. Check back here for your link to buy tickets.

FAN TEXT IS THE NEW FAN MAIL
With Fan Text from AT&T Wireless, you can cheer on your favourites, tell them what you think about their hair styles, clothes, even their song choices. So what are you waiting for? Click here to get your favourite contestant's fan code, and tell your idols your behind them all the way.

5 Many reality TV shows give the public (the audience) the chance to vote for the contestants on the show. What is the idea behind this?

6 This web page wants visitors to the web site to place a vote. How many ways can you vote?

7 The main purpose of this web site is to promote *American Idol*. However, there are also some adverts on the page. This is because companies know that the show is popular and if they advertise here, many people will see their adverts. How many adverts can you see?

8 This web page is trying hard to persuade its visitors to spend money on the official merchandise. Make a list of the **persuasive devices** used on the page.

 Password →

Persuasive devices

A variety of **persuasive devices** can be used to persuade an audience, e.g. use of:
- the second person – 'you'.
- imperatives – 'Vote now!'
- superlatives – 'Who's the best contestant?'.

9 A successful web site makes it easy for visitors to navigate (move around). Write a short paragraph about the **navigation** on this site. Say whether you think the links are easy to find.

Password →

Navigation

In the world of web sites, **navigation** means the ability to 'get around the whole site'.

If visitors to a web site are unable to find their way around, they might click the exit button and leave. On the other hand, if navigation is easy, a visitor might stay on the site for longer.

10 This web page uses colour photographs of scenes from the show.

With a partner, discuss:
➤ who you think decides which photographs appear on the web page
➤ whether the choice of photographs can influence the voting.
Try to give the reasons behind your answers.

11 Deciding what will appear on a web page, and what will not, is called **editing**. Apart from the photographs, can you think of any other parts of a web page which need editing?

Password →

Editing

When a text is prepared for its audience, there is often a process of selecting what will and will not be included. This process is called **editing**.

Editing can involve making decisions about photographs, text, quotations, etc.

Editorials

Next, read the following article written in the US in 2003.

Why Not Reality TV Shows About Real People?

Paul Weyrich

1 The latest idea for a reality show at CBS is called 'The Real Beverly Hillbillies.' If my worst thoughts come true, then this show will be another Hollywood product that shows how divorced its producers are from the rest of America.

2 The idea is that CBS will find a real-life Clampett family, then move them to Beverly Hills and have them set up living quarters in a mansion. Presumably, TV viewers will get their laughs watching a hillbilly family make fools of themselves as they circulate among the 'beautiful people' living life in the fast lane in one of America's most affluent and sophisticated neighbourhoods.

3 Senator Zell Miller is one who decided he would not take this anticipated put-down of rural Americans living in Appalachia sitting down. 'They know the only minority left in this country that you can make fun of and demean and humiliate and put down and hardly anyone will speak up in their defence are hillbillies in particular, and rural people in general. You can ridicule them with impunity. Can you imagine this kind of programme being suggested that would disrespect an African-American family and denigrate a Latino family?'

4 As someone who admires Zell Miller for being a courageous senator, one who will even dissent from time to time against the Politically Correct orthodoxy that has an ironclad grip on the leadership of his party, I'm glad to see him speaking out once more on behalf of rural Americans.

5 CBS has said people should watch the show before they criticize it, a perfectly reasonable enough position in most cases. Only it's hard to avoid a rush to judgement given the very low quality of many of the television shows now airing on the TV networks.

6 My colleague Bill Lind has a better idea than 'The Real Beverly Hillbillies.' Why not take a Hollywood family, locate them in Appalachia, and let them see how decent Americans are able to live meaningful lives centred around family, church and community?

7 But, in the meantime, 'The Real Beverly Hillbillies' will probably wind up on our TV screens in the near future. Fine. Let the reality show turn the cameras on people from Appalachia. I doubt, if it truly is a 'reality' show, that the family will turn out to be the boobs that many people seem to be expecting. Because most people from Appalachia are anything but that.

Glossary

CBS – a US television channel
divorced – detached, separate
Clampett family – the main family of characters in the 1960s US TV show 'The Beverly Hillbillies'
Beverly Hills – a large city in California, home to many film stars
hillbilly – an unsophisticated person from the country

affluent – rich
Senator – a politician in the United States government who has been elected to speak for the people of his or her state
rural – of the country
Appalachia – the area around the Appalachian mountains, which run from Quebec in Canada to the state of Georgia in the USA

demean – put down
ridicule – make fun of
with impunity – without being punished
denigrate – criticize unfairly
dissent ... against – disagree ... with
orthodoxy – accepted practice
ironclad – iron-coated
boobs – fools

1 This article is what we call an **editorial**. How do you think the writer of the editorial (Paul Weyrich) feels about reality TV shows? Sum up your ideas in no more than 20 words.

Password →

Editorials

An **editorial** is an article that gives the newspaper's or news programme's opinions on a particular story or event.

Editorials are also sometimes called 'leader articles'.

2 Editorials, unlike other newspaper articles, are generally written in the first **person**. Find three examples of first person in the editorial.

3 Why do you think editorials are written in the first person. (Hint: think about the aim of this kind of article.)

Password →

Person

Texts can be written in first, second or third **person**.

The first person is often used to give personal opinions, for example,
I think reality TV shows offer great entertainment to the public.

The second person appeals directly to the audience, for example,
You could appear on the next series of 'Big Brother!'

The third person is often used in formal texts, for example,
He/she was very brave during the latest challenge.

4 A good editorial is often a balanced one, presenting more than one point of view. Copy and complete the table below. Put the paragraph numbers in the correct column.

Paragraphs FOR 'The Real Beverly Hillbillies'	Paragraphs AGAINST 'The Real Beverly Hillbillies'

5 Use the **PEE structure** to write a short paragraph about the balance in this editorial.

Password →

PEE structure

PEE stands for Point, Evidence, Explanation. It is a useful method to use when structuring a piece of writing. For example:

In paragraph 5, the writer is against 'The Real Beverly Hillbillies'. (POINT) We know this because he says 'I'm glad to see him speaking out once more on behalf of rural Americans'. (EVIDENCE) This shows that he is on Senator Miller's side and thinks the idea for the new TV show is a bad idea. (EXPLANATION)

6 Editorials often include quotes from other people to back up a viewpoint. Pick out a quote used in this editorial.

By including the name and job title of the person being quoted, a writer can make the argument stronger. This is especially true if the person being quoted is important, for example, a politician.

Look at the following quotes. Which might appear in an editorial and which might not? Be prepared to explain your answers.

Last night, ITV presenter Anthony Jones claimed, 'I love this show. It is fun to watch and be involved in.'

'I am annoyed,' a person said.

A politician replied, 'It is a disgrace!'

Leading news reporter for *The Daily Globe*, Terry Gillingham, commented, 'Shows like this are insulting to the viewers'.

 Editorials may want to challenge the reader's own opinions on the subject. One way to do this is to use **rhetorical questions**. Make a list of the rhetorical questions in this editorial.

Password →

Rhetorical questions

A **rhetorical question** is a question that does not need an answer.

Rhetorical questions are often asked in a dramatic way, in order to draw attention to something. For example, a teacher might say 'Who would have thought that Year 9 would perform so brilliantly?' The teacher does not expect an answer, but is drawing attention to Year 9 performance.

 With a partner, discuss the purpose of each of the rhetorical questions you have listed.

Round-up

With a partner, make a list of:

> ➤ three things you have learned about web sites
> ➤ three things you have learned about editorials.

Over to you

Think up an idea for a brand new reality television show. Then, write and design an attractive web page (not a whole site!) for it.

 Remember!

Think about:
➤ audience – your words and design need to be appropriate
➤ language – appeal to your audience direct using second person and imperatives
➤ text – think about the size, type and colour
➤ pictures
➤ design – make this eye-catching
➤ adverts – which companies might want to sponsor or advertise on your web site?
➤ navigation – are links to other parts of the site clear?

Use a mind map to jot down ideas for your web page.

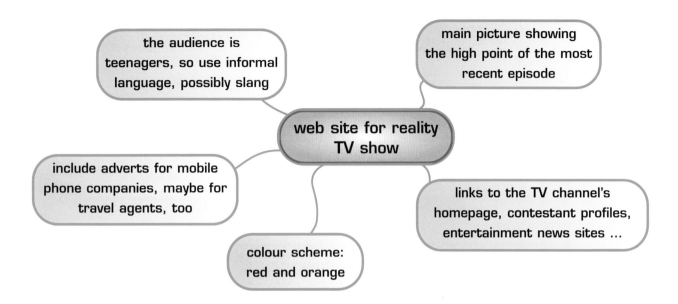

the audience is teenagers, so use informal language, possibly slang

main picture showing the high point of the most recent episode

web site for reality TV show

include adverts for mobile phone companies, maybe for travel agents, too

links to the TV channel's homepage, contestant profiles, entertainment news sites ...

colour scheme: red and orange

 Now follow these steps to complete work on your web page.

1. Decide on the audience for your brand new reality TV show.

2. Think about the layout and look of the page. What is going to go where? How much text/illustration are you going to have?

3. Work on your text. Make the most of each word, especially if space for text is limited.

4. Add your pictures, logos and adverts.

5. Now look at your page as a whole. Is the text too big/small? Do you need to move anything around to make navigation easier? (It might help to show your work to a partner at this stage.)

6. Make any final changes to your web page.

In this unit you will:

➤ look at an information text
➤ identify common features of information texts
➤ write your own information text.

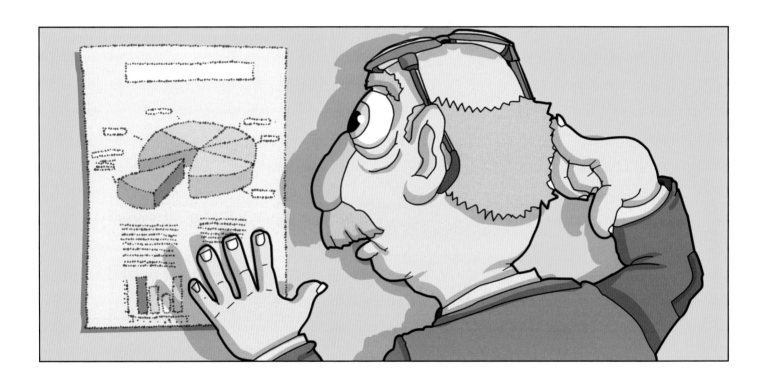

Get started

Information texts are usually easy to identify and straightforward to create. Their main purpose is to inform a reader, so they present facts, usually in a clear, accessible style.

Opposite is a list of features that you often find in information texts. Copy out the list and match up each feature with its correct purpose.

Features

Headings and sub-headings

Tables and diagrams

Third person

Present tense

Simple or compound sentences

Connectives

Facts and figures

Technical vocabulary

Purposes

These are a user-friendly, visual method of getting across complicated information.

These are specialist words that are relevant to the subject.

These link together connecting pieces of information.

This makes the tone of the information sound formal, reliable and unbiased.

This makes information sound up-to-date and therefore relevant.

These divide up the text and show the reader what each part of the text is about.

These ensure that the information is easy to understand, without extra clauses which may confuse the reader.

These give precise information and can back up the text.

Analysing an information text

Read the following information text. It is from a web site about a multivitamin supplement called Multibionta.

Ingredients

Microcrystalline Cellulose, Calcium Ascorbate Granulate 97%, Lactose Monohydrate, Tricalcium Phosphate Anhydrous, Coating: (Shellac, Hydroxypropyl Methyl Cellulose, Acetylated Monoglycerides Povidone Glycerol), Iron (II) Sulphate Hydrate, Vitamin E Preparation (DL- Alpha Tocopheryl Acetate), Glucose, Selenium Yeast, Probiotic Bacteria Powder, Glycerol Monostearate, Nicotinamide, Zinc Oxide, Sodium Carboxymethyl Cellulose, Povidone, Potassium Chloride, Copper (II) Sulphate Pentahydrate, Magnesium Oxide, Calcium Pantothenate, Crospovidone, Vitamin A Preparation, Manganese (II) Sulphate Monohydrate, Magnesium Stearate, Iron Oxide, Vitamin K1 Glucose Trituration, Vitamin D3 Powder, Pyridoxine Hydrochloride, Thiamine Mononitrate, Riboflavin, Colloidal Silicon Dioxide, Cyanocobalamine Glucose Trituration, Folic Acid, Potassium Iodide, Biotin, Chromium (III) Chloride Hexahydrate, Sodium Molybdate Dihydrate.

Nutrients

Vitamins	per Tablet	Minerals	per Tablet
Vitamin A	800µg	Calcium	40mg
Vitamin D	5µg	Phosphorus	16mg
Vitamin E	10mg	Iron	14mg
Vitamin C	60mg	Magnesium	5mg
Thiamin (Vitamin B1)	1.4mg	Zinc	15mg
Riboflavin (Vitamin B2)	1.6mg	Iodine	150µg
Niacin	18mg	Copper	2mg
Vitamin B6	2mg	Manganese	2mg
Folic Acid	200µg	Silicon	2µg
Vitamin B12	1µg	Chromium	25µg
Biotin	0.15mg	Molybdenum	25µg
Pantothenic Acid	6mg	Selenium	30µg
Vitamin K	30µg	Chloride	4.5mg
		Potassium	5mg
Probiotics			
Probiotic Cultures (Lactobacillus acidophilus PA 16/8, Bifidobacterium bifidum MF 20/5, Bifidobacterium longum SP 07/3)	10 million	Energy, Protein, Carbohydrate, Fat	negligible

Lifestyle
Free From Wheat
Free From Gluten
Free From Artificial Colours
Free From Artificial Flavours
Free From Artificial Preservatives

Usage/Storage
RDA = EC Recommended Daily Allowance.
* = RDA not established.

RECOMMENDED DAILY INTAKE: One tablet to be taken with a cold drink each day. Exceeding the daily intake is not recommended. Women who are pregnant or planning a pregnancy should consult their doctor before taking vitamin or mineral supplements. This product contains iron, which if taken in excess, may be harmful to very young children.

KEEP OUT OF SIGHT AND REACH OF CHILDREN. REPLACE LID SECURELY. STORE IN A COOL, DRY PLACE.

Multibionta Probiotic Multivitamin is an advanced formulation complete with Vitamins, Minerals and Probiotics. This breakthrough in nutrition has been developed from worldwide research to produce a formula which supports the immune system to help you cope with stressful days when you can't get all the nutrients you need.

What are Probiotics?

Unlike ordinary multivitamins, Multibionta contains natural Probiotic cultures which help maintain natural balance and support your digestive system.

What are Probiotics?
In our bodies there are billions of friendly bacteria. These friendly bacteria play a vital role in keeping us fit and healthy. These are called Probiotics and they help provide the balance for good health.

What do Probiotics do?
The immune system is our body's natural defence against bad bacteria and infections. Probiotics form a line of defence against the bad bacteria that inhabit our bodies. By doing this, Probiotics help to support our immune and digestive systems to help you cope with every day life. It is important that we have a good level of Probiotics in our bodies at all times for our health and well-being.

Unlike ordinary multivitamins, Multibionta contains natural Probiotic cultures.

Good bugs vs. bad bugs

Did you know there are more than 400 bacterial species that inhabit the large intestine? This may sound alarming but these species are often referred to as 'good' or friendly bacteria.

Good bugs
They work hard in the digestive tract to promote digestion and better absorption of nutrients from your food. They can even help control the more harmful bacteria that live there too.

Bad bugs
The 'bad' bugs are known as pathogens. They produce chemicals that can be toxic to your body and which are often responsible for the more common digestive problems including constipation, diarrhoea, inflammation and chronic conditions like IBS.

If you are wondering how these bugs enter the body, you need to remember that we are surrounded by bacteria and that every day, our bodies are fighting off the bad ones. The good news is that you can easily influence the balance of good and bad bacteria in the gut with what you eat. You can help keep the level of those all important good bacteria high by taking a Probiotic supplement like Advanced Formula Multibionta.

1 How do the headings and sub-headings help you to use the text? Give a specific example of each in your answer.

2 The text includes a table of nutrients. Why is this information presented in this way, rather than in sentence form?

3 Look again at the section under the sub-heading 'Good bugs'.

    a Which words tell you that this section is written in the third person? Make a list.

    b Why has the writer chosen to use the third person here?

    c Which words tell you that this section is written in the present tense?

    d Why has the writer chosen to use the present tense here?

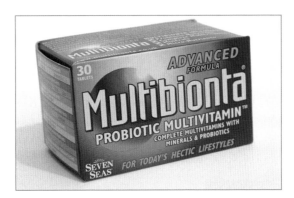

4 Now look at the Multibionta text as a whole. Find an example of a short, simple sentence. Why is it important that this sentence is not long and complicated?

5 There are many facts and figures in this information text. Why?

6 List examples of technical vocabulary. Do you think these words reassure or alienate the reader?

7 Although the main purpose of this text is to inform the reader about Multibionta, it is also trying to persuade the reader to take Multibionta, too.

    a Pick out information that makes the product sound attractive.

    b What persuasive techniques does the text use?

Round-up

With a partner, list four features of information texts. Share your ideas with the rest of the class.

Over to you

Now write your own information text.

Choose one of the following topics:
➤ your favourite football club (perhaps including sections on the ground, the players, history and fixtures).
➤ your school (either focusing on just one area, such as food, sport, or after-school activities, or more generally on all aspects of your school).
➤ your town or area (including information on local transport, activities, town history and shopping).

➔ Remember!

Include some of the following techniques:
➤ Headings and sub-headings
➤ Tables and diagrams
➤ Third person
➤ Present tense
➤ Simple and compound sentences
➤ Connectives
➤ Facts and figures
➤ Technical vocabulary

Plan

Use a mind map like the one below to collect ideas for your information text.

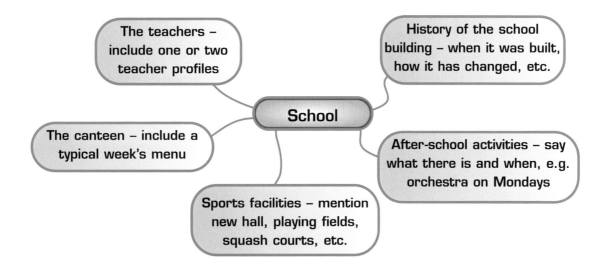

The teachers – include one or two teacher profiles

History of the school building – when it was built, how it has changed, etc.

School

The canteen – include a typical week's menu

After-school activities – say what there is and when, e.g. orchestra on Mondays

Sports facilities – mention new hall, playing fields, squash courts, etc.

1. Decide on how you are going to organize your ideas and your layout. Remember to use headings and sub-headings to divide your text up into manageable chunks.

2. Draft your text. Try to include some of the key features of information texts.

3. Read through your work. Does it sound and look like an information text? Make any changes you think will improve it.

4. Get feedback on your text from a partner. Is there anything you could do to make it even better?

5. Complete a final version of your information text.

Arguing a case

In this unit you will:

➤ look at the persuasive features that can make an argument convincing
➤ write a counter-argument.

Get started

When we argue a case or try to persuade somebody to do something, we use certain techniques to help us sound more convincing. In this unit, you will learn more about these techniques and how to use them to argue a point successfully.

In a group of three, decide who is A, who is B and who is C. Then follow these instructions for two minutes:

A – try to argue that B should buy you a chocolate bar or a packet of crisps at breaktime.
B – listen and argue back.
C – observe and make notes about how A tries to persuade B.

Discuss the persuasive techniques that were used. Can you think of any others?

A leaflet

Read this text from the World Wildlife Fund.

Wildlife Trade

1 **Though they may seem too large and fierce to be threatened, many species are today forced to the edge of extinction. Join with WWF to ensure that our children will know animals like rhinos and tigers as more than zoo attractions.**

2 One of the primary threats to many species is the illegal wildlife trade. Since 1970, for instance, more than 90 percent of the world's wild rhinos have disappeared, slaughtered by the thousands for one primary reason: their magnificent horns. WWF plays a key role in protecting endangered species and their natural habitats through its support of the TRAFFIC Network, the world's largest wildlife trade monitoring program. TRAFFIC works to identify unsustainable trade in wild plants and animals. This vital work includes assisting CITES in identifying problem areas such as loopholes and law infringements and making recommendations about which species should be covered under CITES.

What Can You Do?

3 For more information on illegal wildlife trade and the TRAFFIC Network:
- » Read the TRAFFIC report on Snow Leopard Threats.
- » Read the brochure from TRAFFIC and the U.S. Fish and Wildlife Service on avoiding endangered species in traditional Chinese medicines.
- » Go to the TRAFFIC website.
- » Join WWF.

Say 'NO' to Bad Medicine and Souvenir Buyers

5 Some souvenirs could end up costing a lot more than you paid for them. Think twice before you buy any products made from endangered species, including animal hides and body parts, tortoise-shell, ivory, or coral – they could be illegal. Supporting this damaging trade doesn't just add to the pressure on endangered species, you could also risk having your goods seized when you get home.

6 Also, you can help by becoming a member of WWF! WWF is dedicated to saving endangered species and spaces, including pandas, around the world, and with your help, we can make sure that we leave our children a living planet.

Glossary
extinction – becoming extinct (not existing any more)
monitoring – keeping an eye on
unsustainable – unable to be continued at the same level
CITES – the Convention on International Trade in Endangered
  Species of Wild Fauna and Flora
loopholes – ways of avoiding a law without actually breaking it
infringements – breaking of a law
hides – animal skins

1 What is the World Wildlife Fund arguing against in this text?

2 The writer uses pronouns to appeal directly to the audience, for example 'our children'. Find an example of another pronoun the writer uses (more than once) to involve the reader.

3 Pick out a **rhetorical question** in the argument. What effect does it have?

 Password →

Rhetorical questions

A **rhetorical question** is a question that does not need an answer.

Rhetorical questions are often asked in a dramatic way, in order to draw attention to something. For example, a parent might say to his/her teenage child: 'How many times do I have to tell you to tidy your room?' The parent does not expect an answer, but is drawing attention to the fact he/she is *always* telling the teenager to tackle the mess.

4 Many writers include **statistics** in their arguments. Find one example of statistics in the WWF text. Why do you think this is included?

Password →

Statistics

A piece of information expressed as a number is called a **statistic**.

For example:
The population increased by 50% between the years 1957 and 1983.

5 Texts that argue sometimes use **emotive language** to shock the reader. In Paragraph 2, the writer uses the verb 'slaughtered' rather than 'killed' as it is more powerful. How many other examples of emotive language can you find?

Password →

Emotive language

Writers sometimes choose words to make you feel strong emotions. This is called **emotive language**. Emotive words can be nouns, verbs, adjectives, or adverbs.

For example, 'Traders ransack coral reefs to sell souvenirs to tourists'. Here, 'ransacked' stresses the careless, destructive action of the traders.

6 Adjectives can also add power to an argument.

For example, in Paragraph 2, the adjective 'vital' in the phrase 'this vital work' stresses the importance of the WWF's work, and adds power to the argument.

Find another powerful adjective in Paragraph 2.

7 Look at the bulleted points under the sub-heading 'What Can You Do?'

What kind of sentences does the writer use? Explain their effect.

Imperatives

The **imperative form** of a verb is used to give a command or tell someone to do something.

For example,
  Sit down!

A letter

Imagine this letter is printed in your local paper. Read it through carefully.

Dear Editor,

1   I often ask myself: why do I live in this pathetic town? Whilst neighbouring towns and cities are full of new developments and improvements, our town continues to be left behind. We are a community failing to move with the times and I am ashamed to say I live here.

2   Many towns and cities have been blessed by new housing developments, which not only look modern, but are also attracting new, desirable people into the area. What do we have? Rundown estates where all of the houses look the same: cheap, untidy and uncared for. Gardens are littered with old furniture or broken down vehicles that are slowly rusting. Young children roam the streets half-dressed whilst neighbours argue over broken fences. Would you want to live here?

3   The town centre is old fashioned and dirty. Every other shop is either a charity shop or a discount store. Why can't we attract some of the well-known high street stores? Why should the decent folk have to drive ten miles to another town to buy quality goods or use decent leisure facilities? The answer is simple. Nobody will invest in this town whilst we allow violence, thuggish behaviour and criminal damage to dominate our high street.

4 Furthermore, all of the decent people have moved away leaving only the scum. Every street seems to have its resident gang of yobs who spend their evenings dropping litter, defacing public buildings and/or intimidating innocent citizens such as myself. Discipline is what is needed but the parents are too busy enjoying themselves at the local pub to notice where their children are or what they are doing. As for drugs – the law does not seem to apply to some of our local citizens. Where will it all end?

5 Overall, we live in the most depressing, boring and unfriendly town. I hope somebody at the local council realizes what is happening to our once civilized community and soon. Let us see some money being spent in our area and some effort being put into restoring public pride. Let us see the community standing up to the drug dealers, the joy riders and the hooligans. Finally, let us see a town that is built for the twenty-first century.

Yours faithfully,

Anonymous

Glossary
Editor – the person in charge of a newspaper (also a person who prepares written material for publication)
invest – use money to make a profit, e.g. by lending it in return for interest
defacing – spoiling the surface of
intimidating – frightening by threats
restoring – repairing, mending
Anonymous – a word used to hide a person's real name from the public

1 What is the main argument in this letter? Sum it up in two or three sentences.

2 The writer makes use of rhetorical questions. Find one example and explain why the writer has used it.

3 Writers often use exaggeration to persuade a reader. For example, in Paragraph 4, the writer claims 'all of the decent people have moved away'. Find another example of exaggeration.

4 Writers often list things in threes for emphasis, for example 'cheap, untidy and uncared for'. Find two more examples of the 'list of three' technique.

5 In this letter, the writer uses emotive language. Write down one example and explain the effect it has.

6 Does this letter mostly contain facts or opinions? Use the **PEE structure** to explain how you can tell.

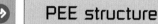
Password →

PEE structure

PEE stands for Point, Evidence, Explanation. It is a useful method when structuring a piece of writing. For example:

In the letter, there are more opinions than facts. (POINT) For example, the writer says 'we live in the most depressing, boring and unfriendly town'. (EVIDENCE) However, to someone else, the same town might feel very different – exciting and friendly. (EXPLANATION)

7 The writer uses a few connectives in this letter. Find them and make a list. What job do they do?

8 Each paragraph in this argument has a particular topic. Copy and complete the grid below. (Use the topic sentences to help you.)

Paragraph	Main topic
1	
2	
3	
4	
5	

Building up a counter-argument.

A counter-argument is the opposite view to a view that has already been expressed.

In the letter, for example, the writer believes his town is failing to move with the times. A counter-argument might be that the town has made some attempt to move with the times by building a new leisure centre and a skating park.

9 With a partner, focus on Paragraph 2 of the letter. Imagine that you live in the same town as the writer, but you disagree with the argument in this paragraph. Discuss ideas for a counter-argument.

10 Using your ideas from Question 9, draft a paragraph of counter-argument to Paragraph 2.
(Hint: if you feel the writer is just giving an opinion or exaggerating a point, say so!)

11 A writer can use connectives to signal a counter-argument to a reader. Look at the connectives/connecting phrases below. Make a list of the ones that signal opposition.

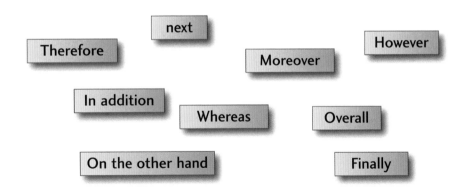

next

Therefore

Moreover

However

In addition

Whereas

Overall

On the other hand

Finally

12 When writing a counter-argument, powerful vocabulary can be used to express personal feelings. You might want to state that you were 'disgusted' or 'outraged' by the anonymous letter.

In pairs, make a list of words that could be used to complete the following sentence.

I found the anonymous letter about our town, which appeared in last week's paper, absolutely ...

Look at the following sentences from the letter. One is a simple sentence, one is a compound sentence, and one is complex.

  a Which is which?
  b Why do you think the author uses all three types?

> 'We are a community failing to move with the times and I am ashamed to say I live here.'
>
> 'Whilst neighbouring towns and cities are full of new developments and improvements, our town continues to be left behind.'
>
> 'The town centre is old fashioned and dirty.'

 List any examples of repetition the writer uses in the letter. Why do you think the writer uses this technique?

 The writer tries to end each paragraph on a powerful note. How does he/she do this?
(Hint: think about the persuasive techniques you are familiar with.)

Round-up

 With a partner, list four persuasive techniques that you could use when writing an argument or counter-argument text. Then share your ideas as a class.

Over to you

 Imagine the anonymous letter was written about the town that you live in. Write a letter of reply to your local newspaper arguing that your town is a great place to live. Include counter-arguments to the points in the anonymous letter.

Remember!

To make your argument convincing, use some of the following techniques:
➤ Rhetorical questions and pronouns (to involve your readers)
➤ Emotive language and adjectives (to add force to what you are saying)
➤ Formal language (avoid slang)
➤ Lists of three
➤ Repetition
➤ Connectives (to signpost the counter-argument)
➤ A variety of sentence types

Plan

Copy and complete the following table to help you plan your counter-argument.

	Ideas for counter-argument
Paragraph 1	
Paragraph 2	
Paragraph 3	
Paragraph 4	
Paragraph 5	
Useful connectives and phrases	

Follow the steps below to complete your counter-argument.

1. Write your introduction (Paragraph 1). Outline your point of view.

2. Write the main part of your argument (Paragraphs 2 – 4). Use the counter-arguments you listed in the table on page 83.

3. Write your conclusion (Paragraph 5). Sum up your feelings.

4. Read through your letter. Check that you have used some of the techniques in the Remember panel.
(Hint: it might be useful to ask a partner for feedback on your letter at this point.)

5. Prepare a final draft of your counter-argument.

Writing essays

In this unit you will:

➤ read and mark examples of essays
➤ improve your ability to write formal essays
➤ give points of view in a balanced way
➤ discuss a range of issues.

Get started

You have already had some practice at writing essays – not just in English, but in other subjects, too. In this unit, you will learn some techniques to make essay writing easier. They will help you feel more confident when writing an essay.

With a partner, make a list of some essays you have written over the last year and which subjects you wrote them in. For example:

History – Why Cromwell won the Civil War
Science – How nuclear power has benefited the world

Discuss which essay you found the most straightforward/difficult to write. Why do you think this was?

Students' essay extracts

The extracts below are from students' Geography essays. Students were given the task 'Explain how the settlement in this area developed' and told to refer to their own town.

As you read, think about which extract you think is strongest.

The first houses built were just huts, but as more people came to work on the river the houses became better. A settlement was built here because there was a river. In Medieval times it was important to have a source of water, both for drinking and washing and for ships to use. More people lived here by 1666, but that was because people left London to come here because of the Plague. The river here helped industry develop as raw materials could be brought in and goods taken out using the river.

Sam

It is thought that the first settlement was built here in the thirteenth century. The river was an important factor, as in those days people relied on the river for many things, including communication. Raw materials for building and the manufacture of goods such as weapons would have been transported to and from the settlement by boat.

The settlement grew in size as cities became crowded and their inhabitants left. As a growing town near the farms in the river plain area, it had access to plenty of food.

Jamie

We have studied how the town grew up. I have learnt that the first place was built about seven hundred years ago. A main reason was the river. Ships and boats brought things and people stayed here because of work. There were lots of farms too and they sent food to sell at the market and that also helped people live there. There is still a market here. You can buy clothes and things as well as food. The town is still growing and there are lots of new houses.

Ayesha

1 In pairs, examine Sam's extract. Think about its strong points and its weaker points. Copy and complete the table below to record your ideas.

Sam's extract	
Strong points	Weak points
	➤ the order is muddled

2 As a pair, put the extracts in order – from most to least successful.

3 Join up with another pair. Discuss which extract you think is likely to score the highest mark and why. Make a list of its strongest points. (These will be your DOs.)

4 Now discuss why the other two extracts are unlikely to score a high mark. Make a list of their weakest points. (These will be your DON'Ts.)

5 Below are some more DOs and DON'Ts for essay writing. (You might already have some of these points in your own lists.) Decide which list each point belongs in.

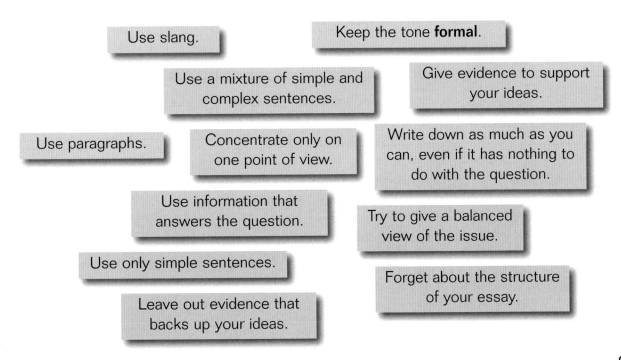

Use slang.

Keep the tone **formal**.

Use a mixture of simple and complex sentences.

Give evidence to support your ideas.

Use paragraphs.

Concentrate only on one point of view.

Write down as much as you can, even if it has nothing to do with the question.

Use information that answers the question.

Try to give a balanced view of the issue.

Use only simple sentences.

Forget about the structure of your essay.

Leave out evidence that backs up your ideas.

Password → **Formal language**

This can be to do with either written or spoken language. It means to use correct words (no slang and few abbreviations) and punctuation in the right places. It is also called Standard English.

Planning an essay

1 An essay plan can help you stay 'on-track' and keep your mind focused on what the question has asked you to do. Sam, Jamie and Ayesha all wrote a plan to help them organize the ideas in their essays.

In pairs, choose one of the extracts on page 86 and try to work out what the plan might have had in it.

2 Find a pair who chose a different essay extract. Compare your plans. What are the main differences between them?

3 In pairs, discuss this essay question:

Are exams a good idea?

4 Copy and complete the table below to record your ideas. A balance of ideas is important. First fill in the first column, then try to think of **counter-arguments** for the second column.

Password →

Counter-arguments

A **counter-argument** is the opposite view to a view that has already been expressed.

For example, if the argument is that exams test a student's knowledge and understanding, then a counter-argument could be that exams only test a small part of a student's knowledge and understanding.

Exams are NOT a good idea	Exams ARE a good idea
Too stressful for young people	Make you focus on what you need to learn

5 You have the ideas. Now you need the evidence to support them and make them more effective. Do some research. You could try:

➤ newspapers and magazines
➤ the Internet
➤ television and radio programmes
➤ other people (friends, parents, teachers)
➤ personal experience.

Aim to find at least one useful piece of evidence for each idea.

Structuring an essay

Now that you have a plan, you need to decide how you are going to organize your ideas.

Introduction

Read the following introduction to a Geography essay about settlement.

> This essay will look at the issue of settlement in this area, and look at reasons why a town has developed here. Some people argue that it was due to the river, while others believe it was because of it being an attractive area to Londoners. Both these points of view will be considered.

1 Using this introduction as a model, draft a short introduction to your essay on exams. Give yourself three minutes.

2 In pairs, compare your introductions. Is there anything you would like to change at this stage?

Paragraphs

Look back as your essay plan. Now you need to organize your ideas into **paragraphs**.

Password →

Paragraphs

Paragraphs are a way of dividing up a text to make it easier to read and understand.

You should begin a new paragraph – shown by starting a new line and indenting from the margin – when:
- ➤ showing a change of speaker
- ➤ introducing a new idea
- ➤ changing the place/subject/time.

Read the paragraph about exams below.

> Exams can be very stressful for students. Many people find they worry so much that they cannot sleep properly when they know they have an exam. This makes it even more stressful because if you are tired, it is not possible to do your best in the exam. Students could find that although they have worked hard and revised, because they have not slept properly, they cannot remember the information they need and so end up with a poor result.

3 This paragraph uses the **PEE structure**. Pick out the point, the evidence and the explanation.

Password →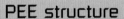

PEE structure

PEE stands for Point, Evidence, Explanation. It is a useful method to use when structuring a piece of writing. For example:

Exams can be very stressful for students. (POINT) Worrying about an exam sometimes means they cannot sleep properly. (EVIDENCE) This is stressful because it is hard to perform well when you are tired, even if you have prepared thoroughly. (EXPLANATION)

This structure helps the reader to understand ideas. It also shows that you can explain your ideas in a balanced way.

4 In the paragraph, what effect does the writer say is caused by stress?

5 How does this support the point and evidence made?

6 Identify the **connectives** in the paragraph. What job do they do?

Connectives

Connectives are words and phrases that link clauses or sentences. They can help to make a text flow better and easier to read.

Examples of connectives are: therefore, firstly, next, moreover, finally, overall, then, despite, although, yet, also, however, whereas, later.

7 The plan you made on page 89 already includes your points and evidence. Now add some ideas for your explanations.

Structure

Essays can be structured in a number of ways. Here are three alternatives:

1
- Deal with each side of the topic separately.
- Focus on all the points, evidence and explanations for one side before you tackle the paragraphs for the other side.
- This structure allows you to keep the ideas quite separate and you can make your case strongly.

2
- Deal with each point and its counter-argument in the same paragraph.
- In each paragraph, use the PEE structure to present one point and its counter-argument.
- This is a more complex structure, but can feel more balanced to the reader.

3
- Take each point in turn and write a PEE paragraph for each side.
- Follow the paragraph pattern For/Against/For/Against, etc.
- This structure shows the reader the range of your ideas, but is less useful for showing how you can compare points.

8 In a group, discuss the different structures. Which structure do you think will be most useful for your essay?
(Hint: be prepared to explain your ideas to the group, but remember that different people will prefer different structures.)

9 Choose a structure. Then arrange your points, evidence and explanations to fit your structure to get an essay outline.

10 Share this essay outline with a partner. Ask if the structure is clear for a reader.

Conclusion

The way you end your essay is as important as your introduction. In the last paragraph, you should try to give your personal **opinion** of the issue. It can also be a good place to sum up what you have tried to say in the essay as a whole.

Password →

Opinion

An opinion is one person's point of view.

For example:
   I think drug abuse must be stopped.

Opinions are different from facts, which are pieces of information that can be proved to be true – for example, 'Some drugs are very dangerous'.

Read the following conclusion.

> Overall, I think that exams can be useful at some times. However, I also think that there should be more chances for students to have work assessed as they go along instead of a result being just on a final exam. I think everyone would benefit from the exam system being changed.

11 How does the writer show that this is his/her personal opinion?

12 The writer repeats the phrase 'I think ...' three times. How could he or she have avoided this repetition?

13 Why should the writer consider using a variety of phrases in his or her writing?

14 What is your personal opinion about exams? Write down three points. You will be able to use these in your conclusion.

Round-up

In a group, discuss what you have learnt about writing an essay.
Answer the following questions:
- ➤ Name three important parts of an essay.
- ➤ Why is a plan useful?
- ➤ Name three useful sources of evidence.
- ➤ When should you start a new paragraph?
- ➤ Why do you need to explain the points you make?
- ➤ What are the different ways to structure an essay?
- ➤ What can you include in the conclusion?

Over to you

Now write your essay to answer the question 'Are exams a good idea?'

→ Remember!

Think carefully about:
- ➤ the overall structure of your essay
- ➤ how you will begin the essay
- ➤ use of paragraphs
- ➤ use of the PEE structure
- ➤ which connectives you will use
- ➤ how you will end the essay.

Use the diagram on page 95 to help you picture the structure of your essay.

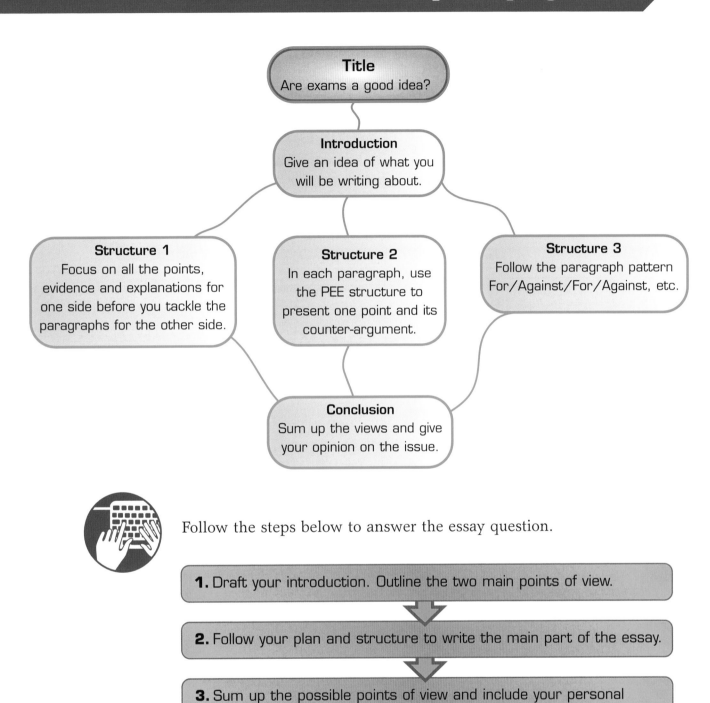

Title
Are exams a good idea?

Introduction
Give an idea of what you
will be writing about.

Structure 1
Focus on all the points,
evidence and explanations for
one side before you tackle the
paragraphs for the other side.

Structure 2
In each paragraph, use
the PEE structure to
present one point and its
counter-argument.

Structure 3
Follow the paragraph pattern
For/Against/For/Against, etc.

Conclusion
Sum up the views and give
your opinion on the issue.

Follow the steps below to answer the essay question.

1. Draft your introduction. Outline the two main points of view.

2. Follow your plan and structure to write the main part of the essay.

3. Sum up the possible points of view and include your personal opinion on exams.

4. Read through your essay. Does it read smoothly? Check that you have covered all the points in your plan.

5. Check for any spelling or punctuation mistakes.

Advice texts

In this unit you will:

➤ look at the main features of advice texts
➤ learn to recognize an authoritative, formal tone
➤ put together paragraphs of an advice text in an appropriate order
➤ write your own advice text.

Get started

Advice texts come in all shapes and sizes. You probably read more of them than you realize. For example, an article in a computer game magazine on how to get to the highest level in a game is an advice text. So is a poster in the gym on how to warm up. Any text which gives you information and recommends something, is an advice text.

Read the statements on page 97. With a partner, use your knowledge of advice texts to decide which ones are true and which are false. Divide them into two lists:

True	False
Advice texts often use a question as a heading ...	

a Advice texts often use a question as a heading, to introduce the topic.

b Advice texts often use imperatives to give commands.

c Advice texts sometimes use bullet points and sub-headings.

d Advice texts are always written in chronological order.

e Advice texts tell a story.

f Advice texts use figurative language, e.g. metaphors and similes.

g Advice texts never include illustrations or diagrams.

h Advice texts can include checklists which summarize what should be done.

i Advice texts never use Standard English.

j Advice texts can be formal or informal.

k Advice texts often use the second person, 'you', to address the reader directly.

l Advice texts often use an impersonal, authoritative tone.

m Advice texts use positive, encouraging words to build up the reader's confidence.

Examining an advice text

Read the text on page 98. Its purpose is to advise people on how to save money.

Pay Yourself First: Save More, Spend Less

1 Saving should be your *top* priority. After you've covered essential monthly expenses –
such as food, rent and utilities – you should put money away before you spend it on
things you want rather than need.

The essence of this lesson is to 'pay yourself first.' That is, get into the habit of putting
5 a fixed amount of your income into savings and/or investments every month before you
decide to spend on something new. The purpose of this is to ensure that your money is
going towards things that are really important, such as the long-term happiness of you
and your family, before you spend it on non-essentials such as a fancy new car, a night
on the town, or a piece of clothing that will just hang in the wardrobe …

10 The key is to make saving a regular habit. Set yourself a goal, and try to save a certain
amount of money each week or month, even if it's only a small amount. Don't worry too
much at first about how much you save, or where you save it; just learn to make it a
habit. Once you start saving on a regular basis, you'll be amazed at how quickly your
nest-egg grows.

15 We all face a constant battle of wills between the Angel of Saving and the Devil of
Spending. Sometimes you need a trick to give the Angel the upper hand. What I do is
deduct 10 percent of every payment I receive – whether it's a pay cheque or just the
repayment of a loan to a friend – and put it into my savings … The Angel of Saving
would say I am rewarding myself with this habit; just as quickly, however, the
20 Devil of Spending reminds me that I now have more money to spend – but I've grown
deaf in that ear …

Your first objective is to build a cushion for emergencies. Your goal should be to save at
least three to six months' worth of living expenses …

Use the money in your current account to pay your daily living expenses, and keep
25 the money in your savings account off-limits …

Once you've saved enough for emergencies, you can then look at saving elsewhere.
You should aim to contribute to tax-free investments, such as National Savings
Certificates, or a cash ISA (Individual Savings Account), a government-sponsored tax-
free savings scheme.

30 Whatever you do, don't spend more than you earn, and don't save your
hard-earned money in the cookie jar: the only interest that money will attract is from the
mice … or a burglar!

From *Money For Life – Everyone's Guide to Financial Freedom* by Alvin Hall

There are eight paragraphs in this text. A to H give a summary of each paragraph, but they are in the wrong order. Copy and complete the grid below, putting the summaries in the correct order. The first one has been done for you.

a Reminds you of the main task, and gives a final piece of advice.
b Gives advice on the first steps towards a savings plan.
c Tells you what steps to take after setting up a savings plan.
d Gives personal advice on how to keep up the habit of saving.
e Gives advice on what your first goal for your savings should be.
f Explains the purpose of saving money: why we should do it.
g Introduces the concept of saving, summarizing the idea of saving money rather then spending it.
h Sums up the main message of the text.

1	Introduces the concept of saving, summarizing the idea of saving money rather than spending it. (g)
2	
3	
4	
5	

 Pick out three time **connectives** in this text and three connectives that link ideas or paragraphs.
(Hint: look at phrases as well as single words.)

Password →

Connectives

Connectives can be words or phrases. They link together sentences and paragraphs.

For example:
   Word connectives – *then, next, first, once, before, after,* etc.
   Phrase connectives – *As a result ..., the purpose of this ..., in the meantime ....*

3 This advice text uses many imperative verbs (action words given in the form of a command, e.g. *'Don't* worry.').

 a List five imperative verbs from the text.
 b Why do you think the author uses them?

4 In this advice text, the author often uses the second **person** ('you') to address the reader. Find some examples and discuss with a partner what effect this has.

 Password →

Person

Text can be written in the first, second, or third **person**, depending on the effect that the writer wants to create.

For example:
 The first person, 'I', or 'we' shows that the writer is speaking personally.
 The second person, 'you', addresses the reader directly.
 The third person, 'he', 'she', 'it', or 'they', are used in impersonal statements.

5 The text also uses the first and third person. Find an example of each and explain why you think the author uses these forms in these instances.

6 Advice texts often use encouraging and reassuring words to make the reader feel positive. Pick out some examples of encouraging and reassuring language in this text.

7 This text uses formal Standard English (which means no slang, and no dialect words or phrases). Why do you think the author chose to write it like this?
 (Hint: think about the intended audience.)

8 In the text, a 'nest-egg' is used to describe a good sized amount of money that someone saves up for the future.

 a List any other specialist vocabulary in the text.
 b Explain what each term means. (You may need to use a dictionary.)

9 Some advice texts include a summary checklist of what should be done. Write one for this text.
(Hint: use bullet points and start each point with an imperative verb.)

> ### Save More Spend Less Checklist
> • Save a certain amount of money each week or month.

Putting together an advice text

Read all the text extracts below. They are notes, adapted from the *SAS Survival Handbook* by John Lofty.

Protection Against Sharks

⇨ Risk is great to anyone in the water.
⇨ Not a foregone conclusion that a shark attack will occur.
⇨ Shark repellent may not be 100% effective –only use when absolutely necessary – you can use it only once.

On a raft or boat:

⇨ Don't fish when sharks are around and don't throw waste overboard (including excrement and fish offal). Let go of baited hooks.

⇨ Do not trail arms or legs in the water.

⇨ If a shark threatens to attack discourage it with jabs to the snout with a paddle or pole. Remember – a large shark could also take a bite out of a boat or raft.

In the water:

⇨ If sharks are present try to avoid passing body wastes, which could attract the sharks' interest. If you must urinate do it in short, sharp spurts and allow it to dissipate between spurts. Collect faecal matter and throw it as far away from you as possible. If you vomit try to hold it in the mouth and reswallow it, but if this proves impossible throw it as far away as possible.

⇨ If it is necessary to swim use strong, regular strokes, avoiding schools of fish.

⇨ If a group of people are threatened they should bunch together and face outwards. To ward off attack kick outwards and punch out with a stiff arm using the heel of the hand – like a sports 'hand-off.'

⇨ Make loud noises by slapping the water with cupped hands. Put your head under the water and shout. These measures are more effective with a group but can work even when you are alone and under attack. If you have a knife, be prepared to use it. Let the shark take it fully in the snout, or go for the gills and eyes.

Use these notes to put together an advice text on how to protect yourself against sharks.

1 First, draw up a plan. You will need a title, introduction and conclusion. Decide where you will put advice for people in the water, then for people in a boat or raft. You may want to include a checklist.

2 Write out your advice text. These ideas might help you:

➤ Put the title in the form of a question.

➤ You may wish to include some simple diagrams or artwork.

➤ Think carefully about how to link your paragraphs together.

➤ Write in formal Standard English.

➤ Use imperatives where you want to sound authoritative.

➤ Include encouragement and reassurance.

Round-up

With a partner, think of five key features that you often find in advice texts. Discuss, then list them in order of importance.

Over to you

In an exam, you may be asked to write an advice text from scratch. Using all that you have learnt in this unit, have a go at writing your own advice text.

Choose one of the following topics, or think up one of your own:
> How to get and keep a part-time job.
> Advice for keeping up to date with homework and revision.
> Organizing the perfect party.
> Caring for a pet.
> How to become a better footballer/console game player/ snowboarder.
> Becoming an expert texter.

→ Remember!

Advice texts often use:
> the second person, to appeal directly to the reader
> formal Standard English
> imperatives
> specialist vocabulary
> words of encouragement and reassurance
> bullet points
> connectives to link sentences and paragraphs
> checklists

Plan

First brainstorm ideas to include in your advice text. You might find it helpful to jot them down in a mind map.

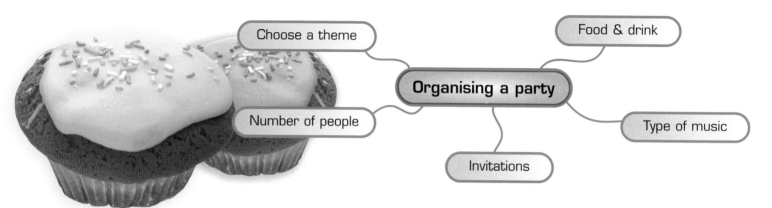

Next, plan the order of your paragraphs, including an introduction, checklist and conclusion.

Follow the steps below to write your advice text in full.

1. Write your first draft.

2. Read it through, and give it to a partner for his or her comments.

3. Check you have stuck to your plan and that your paragraphs are linked together.

4. Refer back to the Remember panel to remind you of key features of advice texts.

5. Amend your draft, checking punctuation and spelling.

6. Write out a final presentation of your work.

Description

In this unit you will:

- ➤ learn how to use rhetorical devices
- ➤ read some humorous non-fiction
- ➤ write descriptive paragraphs.

Get started

By now, you will have had some experience of both reading and writing descriptions. With a partner, talk about what makes a description interesting for a reader. Think about a description that you know and like. What makes it memorable, or unusual?

When writing a description, what might you use to help your audience build up a good picture in their heads? With a partner, jot down your ideas.

1. powerful, unusual words
2. striking images
3. metaphors
4.

Rhetorical devices

Most of the items on the list you drew up on page 105 can probably be described as rhetorical devices. It is important to know the meaning of this term as you could be asked to write about **rhetorical devices** in a text or even to use them yourself in a writing task.

Password →

Rhetorical devices

A **rhetorical device** is a way of speaking or writing, which helps to impress or persuade your audience.

For example: metaphors, similes, alliteration, assonance, repetition, rhetorical questions, onomatopoeia, and noun phrases are all rhetorical devices.

1 Check what you know about the rhetorical devices listed below by pairing up each device with its definition. Copy out the pairs.

Rhetorical devices

Metaphor

Alliteration

Imagery

Simile

Onomatopoeia

Repetition

Noun phrase

Rhetorical question

Definitions

Words intended to copy the actual sounds heard, e.g. *Plop.*

Words chosen to create a picture in the mind of the reader, e.g. *Fog oozed and slithered its way across the defenceless estate.*

A noun, pronoun or group of words that work in the same way as a noun, e.g. *the best team in the world.*

Compares two things using the words 'like' or 'as', e.g. *Her temper was like a volcano.*

A question to which an answer is not really expected, but which focuses on an issue, e.g. *Who will protect children from the menace of internet perverts?*

Repeating the same consonant sound at the beginning of words, e.g. *Four fancy feet.*

Compares two things by saying one thing is another, e.g. *He was a monster towards his mother!*

Using the same word or phrase to give extra emphasis, e.g. *Give us peace, give us hope.*

2 In pairs, think up another example of each rhetorical device. Try to make it interesting, funny or unusual, so that it would entertain a reader.

Using the senses

As well as using rhetorical devices, many writers focus on the senses to try and give the reader a clear feeling of what he or she is trying to describe.

Read the extract on page 108. It is about a visit to a tribe in New Guinea.

I walked into deep mud, suddenly sinking to my hips in wet ooze which cloyed around my legs. I had to struggle quite hard to get back on to firm ground. After floundering out, hot, wet and mud-covered, I went and lay in the stream to wash the mud off …

When the Kraimbits saw me arrive they began calling to each other in excitement and many came running through the village. It was a wonderful welcome; I shook hands with everyone and couldn't stop smiling … They took me to a shade-shelter, brought fruit for refreshment, and we all sat down together … Five old men began playing their sacred bamboo 'flutes' … they danced in circles … blowing through the bamboo to produce mellow, braying harmonies…

In the late afternoon the villagers went to decorate themselves, painting coloured mud ochres on their bodies and shaking out their head-dresses of fur and feathers. I went to wash at a small, cool spring in the sago-palm forest, using a coconut-shell to scoop up the water and pour it over myself.

Adapted from *The Crocodile's Bite* by Christina Dodwell

1 Think about which senses the writer uses to give the reader a picture of the visit. Copy and complete this table.

Sense	Evidence
Taste/smell	
Touch	
Sound	
Sight	

2 The writer describes two types of 'feelings', the physical sort and the emotional sort. Complete this description of the emotions felt by the author and the tribe:

At the start of the extract the writer seems to feel .... but when she arrives in the village her mood changes. She becomes .... The people she is visiting are .... They show their feelings by .... and .... By the end of the extract the mood has changed again and the writer seems ....

Over to you

Now it is your turn to write a description in which you use your senses.

First, think of a place – a room, a house, a street, a town – that you know well. Close your eyes and 'see' the chosen place in your mind. Imagine you are standing or walking around that place and think about what you would experience while you are there.

Try to write about five paragraphs, one for each sense. Follow the steps below.

1. Start by writing about what you can *see*. Include details about colours, objects and movement.

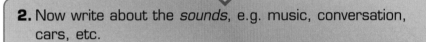

2. Now write about the *sounds*, e.g. music, conversation, cars, etc.

3. Follow the sounds with smells, e.g. fumes, scent, BO!

4. Taste can be a tricky sense to include, but you could associate it with smell, e.g. 'I could smell the roasted beef in the oven and almost taste the succulent meat ...'.

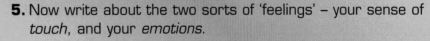

5. Now write about the two sorts of 'feelings' – your sense of *touch*, and your *emotions*.

Check that your description is linked together by suitable connectives to guide the reader around your place.

Swap your work with a partner and discuss how successful your descriptions are at building up a picture for the reader.

Humour in non-fiction

Using your senses is only part of the skill in writing descriptions. To make a description entertaining, some writers also use humour.

Read the extract below, which is part autobiography and part travel writing. Pete McCarthy has gone to Ireland to try and trace where his family came from. He visits a monastery where pilgrims go to feel closer to God. There are strict rules about behaviour – one of them involves having to go barefoot.

> Walking along the pathway towards the first bed, the slap of bare sole on wet concrete was refreshing, though I could see how it might grate after a while. Suddenly two priests walked past me, all in black, smiling.
>
> And wearing shoes.
>
> So we're not in this together, then? They're in charge, and we're in pain. I wonder if they sidle up and give you a sly stamp on the toes if you're not performing up to scratch. Thank God we didn't have to go barefoot at school. There would have been carnage. Teachers would have queued to jump from the tops of cupboards in steel-heeled clogs, crushing our little pink toes like jelly babies. Speaking of feet, I remember one freezing and rainy February day being told the weather was too bad for rugby. A sigh of relief went round the changing room. 'Get changed for a four-mile cross-country run instead' said the teacher in charge. So Mike O'Neill presented him with a letter from his father, a doctor, saying he had a septic foot.
>
> 'Okay, O'Neill,' said the teacher, 'get changed for a four-mile cross-country hop'.

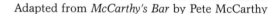

Adapted from *McCarthy's Bar* by Pete McCarthy

1 Pick out a simile the writer has used. In what why is it humorous?

2 Pick out an example of each of the following rhetorical devices and explain their effect:

a alliteration
b rhetorical question
c onomatopoeia.

3 One way of creating humour is through **exaggeration**. Where does the writer use exaggeration to create an extreme picture in the reader's mind? (Hint: look at his thoughts about teachers.)

Password →

Exaggeration

Exaggeration is when something is made to sound more extreme than it really is.

For example:
When my aunt scowls, she looks so scary it makes the milk turn sour.

It is not really possible for a scowl to make milk turn sour, but it gives an idea of the aunt's extremely offensive look.

4 In the first sentence the writer uses 'sole' and 'grate' to create more than one image in the reader's mind. Explain both meanings.

5 The short sentence 'And wearing shoes.' is set on a line of its own. Why has the writer done this and what effect does it have?

6 Why does the writer make the sentence beginning 'So Mike O'Neill ...' a complex one? (Hint: think about the extra information that is included between the commas.)

7 Which senses does the writer use? Pick out examples and say which sense is involved.

8 Which bits of this description made you smile? Explain to your partner why you found them funny. (Remember that what is funny to one person is not necessarily funny to another.)

Irony

Like exaggeration, **irony** is a form of humour found in some non-fiction descriptions. Irony is an entertaining way of making the reader 'read between the lines' to discover what the writer really thinks.

Password →

> ## Irony
>
> Irony is a humorous way of speaking, or writing, in which the speaker, or writer, says the opposite of what he or she really means.
>
> For example:
> I wrote and told my aunt how thrilled I had been to receive her gift of a personalized, hand-knitted, orange jumper for my 14th birthday, instead of the impersonal £5 note she usually sent.

Read the extract below. It is part of an essay, written by a student.

THE PLACE I HATE MOST

Where is the place I most hate? The lower school dining room! It is painted in an attractive shade of cat-sick green with dried-blood red for the floor tiles. I have spent hours of torture in there. I can still see the lines of kids queuing for lunch, kicking and shoving, shouting and pushing to get to a better position. I was always small for my age so was the victim of these 'lunch-line bullies' on many occasions. I carry the scars on my hands of the times I was trampled over, by bigger kids acting like herds of elephants, on their way to the front of the queue. I can smell in the air the delightful scent of burning boiled potatoes mixed with the delicious aroma of last weeks reheated curry. The body smells from the other pupils adds to the lovely atmosphere, especially those who've done PE last lesson and are still sweaty and sticky from the exercise.

9 List some examples of irony in this text. Remember, irony means the opposite of what is actually said. Your list might start like this:

> • 'an attractive shade of cat-sick green'
> • 'the delightful scent of burning boiled potatoes'

10 Beside each example of irony, write down what you think the writer's real opinion is.

11 What other rhetorical devices does the writer use? Pick out one example of each of the following:

    a a rhetorical question
    b exaggeration
    c a simile
    d alliteration.

12 With a partner, try to continue this piece of writing. Keep the same humorous tone, using irony, exaggeration and other rhetorical devices. (Hint: think about focusing on the senses to give more detail.)

Round-up

In pairs, test each other on your understanding of some rhetorical devices used in descriptions. Answer these questions:

    ➤ What is onomatopoeia? (Explain it, then give an example.)
    ➤ What is alliteration?
    ➤ What are rhetorical questions and why are they used?
    ➤ Which senses could you use to describe a place?
    ➤ Give two different meanings of the word 'feeling'.

Over to you

You are now going to write a description using some of the writing techniques that you have studied in this unit.

The title of your description is to be 'A frightening place'.

> ### ➡ Remember!
>
> Descriptions may:
> ➤ use rhetorical devices to entertain the reader
> ➤ appeal to some or all of the five senses
> ➤ use exaggeration and irony for humour
> ➤ use a mix of long and short sentences, for effect
> ➤ be written by a first person narrator ('I') or a third person narrator ('he', 'she' or 'it')
> ➤ focus on emotions as well as physical things.

Plan

Jot down your ideas in a mind map, like the one below. Replace the questions with your own ideas.

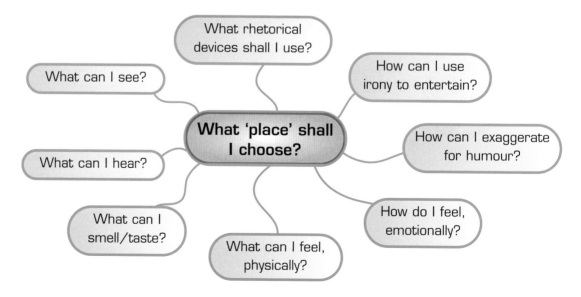

Now write your description, following the steps below.

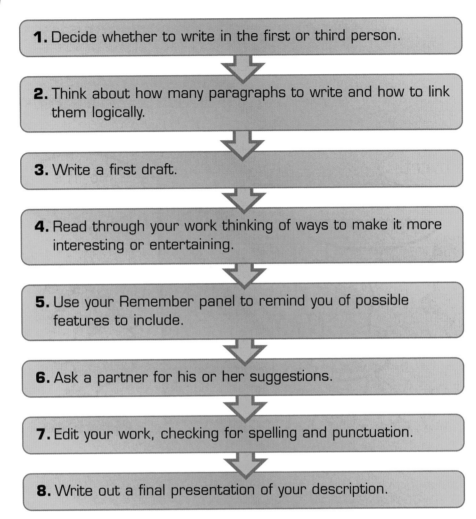

1. Decide whether to write in the first or third person.

2. Think about how many paragraphs to write and how to link them logically.

3. Write a first draft.

4. Read through your work thinking of ways to make it more interesting or entertaining.

5. Use your Remember panel to remind you of possible features to include.

6. Ask a partner for his or her suggestions.

7. Edit your work, checking for spelling and punctuation.

8. Write out a final presentation of your description.

Remember that you are writing a description, not a story!

In this unit you will:

➤ revise the features of different types of non-fiction texts.

Get started

As you already know, there are many different types of non-fiction texts. They are written for different purposes (reasons) and for different audiences (readers). In this unit, you will revise the different types of non-fiction texts, testing your knowledge of the key features of each type.

1 With a partner, make a list of the different purposes of non-fiction texts. Your list might begin like this:

> Purposes of non-fiction texts
> 1. to inform
> 2. to persuade
> 3.

2 Next to each item on your list, write an example of each sort of text. Your list might begin like this:

> 1. to inform, e.g. an entry in an encyclopaedia
> 2. to persuade, e.g. an advert in a magazine
> 3.

Identifying text types

Some non-fiction texts have more than one purpose. For example:
- ➤ a magazine advert might try to **persuade** you to buy the product on show, but also give you **information** about the product.
- ➤ a web site page might offer **information** about the latest fashions and also give **advice** on how to wear certain clothes.

1 With a partner, test how quickly you can spot different text types. Follow these steps:

- ➤ Copy out the grid below.
- ➤ Read the extracts A to H on pages 118 to 120.
- ➤ Fill in the *second* column (the first has been done for you). Remember, some texts might contain a mix of types.

Text types	Extract(s)	Audience
Information	B	
An argument		
Explanation		
Entertainment		
Instruction		
Advice		
Review		
Persuasive text		

A kinda Portuguese custard pie

Caramel

1 big handful of caster sugar
3 tablespoons of water

First place the sugar and water in a pan.
Next, bring to the boil and gently agitate until golden brown. *At this point it will be hotter than hot – don't even think about tasting it!* No kids allowed. Dribble the mixture randomly over your custard tarts – it will bubble and cool to a crisp caramel. Fantastic!
Oh yeah – place the pan in the sink and half fill with water before boiling it up again – you'll have no grief washing it up.

From *The Return of the Naked Chef* by Jamie Oliver

Dublin Castle

For seven hundred years, Dublin Castle embodied English rule as the headquarters of the viceroy. Built by the Anglo-Normans in the early thirteenth century, it was the key element of their walled city and served their successors well, withstanding all attempts to take it by force.

From *The Rough Guide to Dublin*

The Fellowship of the Ring

An extraordinary book. It deals with a stupendous theme. It leads us through a succession of strange and astonishing episodes, some of them magnificent, in a region where everything is invented: forest, moor, river, wilderness, town, and the races which inhabit them.

From *The Observer*

Volcanoes

When an ocean plate collides with a continental plate, it is forced down under the land mass and starts to melt. This forms magna that rises through the continental plate to create volcanoes.

From *Volcanoes* by Jenny Wood

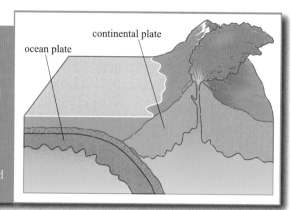

E

Assessing your diet!

Nutritionists advise that in order for the body to function at its optimum it needs a well balanced diet which should include carbohydrates, protein, fats, minerals and vitamins. However, it is only by eating a variety of foods in sensible proportions that we can obtain the correct amount of nutrients needed to maintain good health.

The three basic rules regarding food are that:
- It should nourish the body
- Help safeguard health
- Whenever possible play a role in helping fight against ailments and disease.

From *Get Fit For Summer* by Christine Green

F

The Stunning Yorkshire Dales

Are you wanting the holiday of your lifetime? Then, look no further!

For a fantastic, fun-filled holiday, take the journey of a lifetime into the beautiful and breathtaking setting of the Yorkshire Dales. This spectacular and stunning location is sure to bring you and your family a holiday to be envied by all those around. Whatever you are looking for in a holiday, be it thrills or relaxation, you can be sure to find it here!

G

Get Active! Get a life!

Today, young adults do not know how lucky they are! They have a range of exciting and innovative leisure opportunities at their feet and still they moan, 'there isn't anything to do'. Well, I say they should get up off of their backsides and get wise! Lazy behaviour will only lead to lazy minds. Yes ... I see that some activities available to them might cost a bit of money – but not all! It is only apathy that nurtures this lazy attitude.

H

WELL IF IT ISN'T BULLY BENSON FROM KING STREET JUNIOR SCHOOL! REMEMBER ME ?— "WEEDY WILSON"

From *The Victim's guide to ... the dentist* by Roland Fiddy

2 Now decide on the intended **audience** for each text and fill in the third column in your grid. Remember to think about:

➤ age, gender, specialist interests, etc.
➤ the complexity of the writing – this can give you a clue as to the audience. Short, simple sentences and easy vocabulary is often aimed at a young audience. Complex sentences with sophisticated, specialist vocabulary are usually aimed at an older, knowledgeable audience.

Quiz about stylistic features

Each text type has its own list of stylistic features. These are like ingredients in a recipe. Sometimes a writer decides to leave out one of the ingredients, or add something else, depending on the final result he or she wants.

With a partner, read the lists on the next page and decide which text type each one belongs to. If you get stuck, refer back to some of the Extracts A to H to help you match the features to the correct text types.

List 1

This text type often uses:
- the second person to address the reader directly: 'you'
- a mix of instruction, explanation, persuasion and information
- carefully chosen language to match audience needs
- alternatives for the reader to consider
- a tone which is authoritative, but also encouraging and reassuring
- design features to help relay the message clearly, e.g. bullet points and sub-headings.

List 2

This text type often uses:
- the present tense
- the third person voice, to sound authoritative and impersonal
- clear layout (sub-headings, topic sentences, illustration, captions)
- vocabulary and sentence structures suited to a particular audience.

List 3

This text type often uses:
- rhetorical questions
- exaggeration/superlatives
- repetition/rhyme and alliteration
- imperatives
- a mix of second and third person
- an eye-catching design.

List 4

This text type often uses:
- a clear introductory statement about the topic
- facts and opinions
- connectives
- a clear sequence and structure
- quotations
- a conclusion that sums up the writer's opinion.

List 5

This text type often uses:
➤ the present tense
➤ the third person to sound authoritative
➤ sequence (to link points clearly)
➤ technical/specialized vocabulary
➤ labelled diagrams and illustrations.

List 6

This text type often uses:
➤ a clear opening statement
➤ a summary of what happens (but not the ending)
➤ personal opinions which consider strengths and weaknesses
➤ recommendations about audience
➤ a rating device.

List 7

This text type may use:
➤ some sort of humour, e.g. word puns or irony
➤ descriptive writing – to create context and setting
➤ illustration.

List 8

This text type generally uses:
➤ imperative verbs
➤ a clear sequence
➤ connectives
➤ accompanying illustrations
➤ measurements and quantities
➤ short, clear sentences
➤ adverbs.

The reading paper

The reading paper is worth 32 marks of your overall Key Stage 3 English test mark, so knowing what to expect and how to answer the questions is important.

You will have fifteen minutes at the beginning of the test to read three extracts (which are linked by a common theme). Then you will have one hour to answer approximately fifteen questions. Each of these questions will be worth between 1 and 5 marks. You can judge the importance of each question by the number of marks it is worth and also by the amount of space you have to write your answer.

Read the statements below. Then decide whether each one should be listed as a DO or a DON'T. Complete the table on page 124.

Spend more time on questions worth 5 marks than questions that are worth 1 mark.

Give up if you can't answer the first few questions.

If a question has bullet points, focus on each one in order.

Read the questions carefully and think: What do I have to do? Where do I have to look? It may help to underline key words in the question.

Use short quotations that are relevant to the question.

Use the reading time to think about the purpose of the text and how it is written, e.g. Is the writer trying to persuade me? Has the writer used rhetorical questions or pronouns to involve the reader? What effect does that semi-colon have?

Ignore the reading time as it is boring and pointless.

If a question asks for an explanation, write it in your own words rather than just repeat a quotation.

If a question has bullet points, ignore them.

DOs	DON'Ts
Spend more time on questions ...	

The Shakespeare paper

This paper is worth 18 marks. You will have 45 minutes to write about two extracts.

The question may ask you about:
- ➤ a character, (this could include a question that asks you to write as though you are that character, e.g. Macbeth),
- ➤ a theme,
- ➤ the language
- ➤ it may ask you to plan how you would direct a scene.

Look at the following points, then select five of them to complete a postcard to a friend who is also doing their KS3 English test. (Follow the postcard layout on page 125.)

- ➤ When using quotations, follow the PEE structure.
- ➤ Make sure you write about both extracts.
- ➤ The marker will be impressed if you tell the story of the play in your answer.
- ➤ Select relevant quotations that are not too long.
- ➤ Don't just describe what characters do – comment on how an audience may react.
- ➤ The longer the quotation, the better it is.
- ➤ Comment on features of language that tell us something about character or action.
- ➤ Use lots of quotations – you don't need to comment on them.
- ➤ Read and revise the whole play.
- ➤ Tell the examiner about the life of William Shakespeare.

Dear Tom,

You may find the following tips helpful in your KS3 English exam:

- •

- •

- •

- •

- •

Good luck and see you soon,

. . . .

The writing tasks

The writing tasks make up half of your final English mark, so it is worth preparing yourself well for them. You will have to complete a shorter and a longer writing task.

Use the following bank of words to complete the sentences on page 126. The sentences make up a list of top tips.

plan punctuation sentences paragraph
connectives spelling vocabulary

Top Tips

1. _____ the written tasks, paying attention to the audience and purpose that you are writing for. (So ask yourself: Am I writing to a head teacher or a friend, etc? Am I writing to argue or entertain, etc?)

2. An examiner will be looking to see if you have used a range of _____. (So ask yourself: Have I used commas to mark clauses? Have I used question marks or exclamation marks if it is appropriate?)

3. Link paragraphs and sentences using _____.

4. Each _____ should have a main point and then detail that supports or develops that main point.

5. A wide _____ will impress an examiner.

6. Using a variety of simple, compound and complex _____ will show that you can control the pace and level of your work.

7. Leave time in the exam to proof-read your work for _____ mistakes and other errors.